JAMES MᶜNAIR's
BEEF
COOKBOOK

Photography by Patricia Brabant

Chronicle Books • San Francisco

Printed in Japan

Library of Congress
Cataloging-in-Publication Data
McNair, James K.
James McNair's beef cookbook.
Includes index.
1. Cookery (Beef) I. Title.
II. Title: Beef cookbook.
TX749.5.B43M37 1989
641.6'62
89-7335
ISBN 0-87701-591-0
ISBN 0-87701-583-X (pbk.)

Distributed in Canada by
Raincoast Books
112 East Third Avenue
Vancouver, British Columbia V5T 1C8

10 9 8 7 6 5 4 3 2 1

Chronicle Books
275 Fifth Street
San Francisco, California 94103

For Patricia Brabant, with deep appreciation for so gorgeously
photographing my last twelve books and, more importantly, for being
such a good friend.

Produced by The Rockpile Press, San Francisco and Lake Tahoe

**Art direction, prop and food styling, and book design by
James McNair**

Editorial production assistance by Lin Cotton

Photographic assistance by Bruce Bennett and Carrie Loyd

Kitchen assistance by Glen Carroll

**Typography and mechanical production by Cleve Gallat and
Don Kruse of CTA Graphics**

CONTENTS

INTRODUCTION   5

RAW   11

GRILLED & BROILED   19

ROASTED & BAKED   41

SAUTÉED, PANFRIED, & STIR-FRIED   55

BRAISED & SIMMERED   71

INDEX   94

ACKNOWLEDGMENTS   96

INTRODUCTION

During the past few years of increased interest in nutrition, some people predicted that beef would disappear from the American diet. Fortunately for those of us who enjoy this highly satisfying food, beef remains popular. Our choice of cuts, cooking methods, and serving sizes has changed in light of sound nutritional advice, however.

From my youth, I remember my daddy barbecuing enormous, thickly cut steaks that literally overlapped the plate edges. Now, like millions of others, my whole family opts for smaller portions prepared in lighter ways. American cooks have learned especially valuable lessons from Asian cuisines, in which beef is used to add its special flavor to dishes rather than dominate a meal.

The beef industry is to be saluted for awakening to the fact that health-savvy consumers intend to eat less fat. Ranchers have begun producing leaner cattle that spend more time munching on green grass and hay and less time in the feed lots that produced the well-marbled meat so prized by past generations. Today beef cattle have 40 percent less fat than cattle did three decades ago and their meat is about 10 percent leaner. At the market, beef is trimmed more thoroughly and more emphasis is placed on leaner cuts.

All of the dishes in this book are personal favorites prepared with the leanest cuts of beef, thus you won't find recipes calling for fatty briskets and short ribs. Despite the fact that they are relatively low in fat, I've also decided to forgo cholesterol-rich liver and other innards that can conceal concentrations of potentially harmful toxins.

Though some readers will continue to eat larger helpings than suggested, my servings are calculated at about three ounces of cooked meat per person, the portion size recommended for the average individual by most nutritionists. In many instances, I've reduced the added fats by altering the traditional cooking methods.

Now, read on and enjoy delicious beef with a clear conscience and in good health!

Keep servings to 3 ounces per person; this is a piece of meat about the size of a deck of playing cards. To achieve this portion, start with 4 ounces of raw boneless meat.

Select one of the leanest cuts of beef: tenderloin, sirloin, top round, eye of round, round tip, or top loin.

Choose petite steaks or smaller cuts, or share a larger cut.

When no small steaks are on the menu, select a beef appetizer as a main course.

Cook or order broiled, grilled, or roasted beef; serve or order sauces on the side and use judiciously.

Trim away visible fat before eating.

Marinate beef in wine or lemon juice instead of oil, or pat it with a dry seasoning mixture of herbs and spices and let stand to impart flavor.

After browning crumbled ground beef for a casserole or other dish, place it in a colander, rinse briefly with hot water to wash away excess rendered fat, and drain well.

Cook chili, soup, stew, or spaghetti sauces made with beef a day in advance of serving and chill. Not only do they usually taste better when there has been more time for the flavors to blend, but you also have a chance to skim off any solid fat that collects on top.

Beef Nutrition

A good case for purchasing lean beef cuts is illustrated by the fact that a 3-ounce serving of cooked trimmed lean beef has only 200 calories, with some cuts containing even a bit less. A similar portion of traditionally desirable well-marbled steak jumps to about 300 calories. Of course, sauces and cooking fats increase the caloric count.

Protein makes up about 20 percent of beef calories. Three ounces of cooked beef provide 20 to 30 grams of protein, from 40 to 60 percent of the total daily protein requirement. As a daily source of protein, the U.S. Department of Agriculture's *Dietary Guidelines for Americans* recommends two 3-ounce servings of low-fat protein: lean meat, poultry, fish, or a nonmeat alternative such as dried beans or eggs. Most nutritionists advise that red meat be the choice from this group no more than once a day, preferably only several times a week. The body makes better use of two small servings taken at different times during the day than it does of a single 6-ounce portion eaten at one meal. Since protein is not stored in the body, an excess intake of protein is burned away as an expensive energy source or is converted to stored fat.

Fat accounts for about 50 percent of the calories in well-trimmed beef, which is higher than some other meats but still a smaller percentage than found in whole milk cheese. The American Heart Association recommends that no more than 30 percent of the average person's daily calories come from fat. Translated into usable information, this means that a daily diet of 1,500 calories would allow a total of 50 grams of fat (based on 9 calories for every gram of fat). At the leanest end, a typical serving of cooked and trimmed roast eye of round contains a total of 5.5 grams of fat; at the other end of the scale, broiled supermarket-variety ground beef contains about 17.9 grams of fat per serving.

We've all heard a lot about the supposed high cholesterol content of beef, which is found in about the same quantity in both lean and fatty cuts. In fact, however, the news is not all bad. Typically, a 3-ounce serving of beef, prepared without excessive additional cooking fats, contains 60 to 90 milligrams of cholesterol, about one-fourth of the total daily intake recommended by the American Heart Association. Over half of the beef fat is mono- or polyunsaturated and new evidence even points to some benefits from beef cholesterol.

Monounsaturated oleic acid in beef is the same fatty acid found in olive oil and thought to be highly beneficial in Mediterranean diets. It does not raise serum cholesterol. Surprisingly, stearic acid, one of the main saturated fats found in beef, behaves in the same fashion as oleic acid.

Around the time I started this book, with just a tinge of guilt haunting me about writing on red meat, I was thrilled to read a *New York Times* report by Jane Brody, America's current fitness guru. She reported the early findings of a new study on stearic acid.

It now appears that both stearic and oleic acids may actually help lower cholesterol levels in the blood, in similar fashion to the much-touted omega-3 oils of fatty fish. The study also showed that stearic acid may help moderate the cholesterol-raising effects of other saturated fats in beef.

Nutritional analysts were quick to react to the report, however. The consensus was that we should not overindulge in red meat until further studies back up these preliminary findings.

More good news for beef eaters is the fact that it is rich in vitamins B_6 and B_{12}, as well as iron and zinc, important minerals often absent from meatless diets. The iron in beef is in a form that is highly absorbable by the body.

THE LEANEST CUTS

These cuts are called for in most recipes in this volume.

SHORT LOIN: Tenderloin is cut into fillet steaks, filets mignons (or petite fillets), medallions, tournedos, tips, or kabob pieces. Top loin is cut into London broil, New York, Delmonico, club, or strip steaks.

SIRLOIN: Cut into sirloin steaks, London broil, or kabob pieces, or ground.

ROUND: Top round is cut into roasts, London broil, or steaks; eye of round is cut into steaks or roasts; the tip is cut into steaks or into pieces for kabobs or stews. Any type of round may be sold ground.

I've also included a few recipes calling for flank steak, which contains more than the recommended limit of 30 percent fat. Boneless cuts from this list can be substituted for flank if you must restrict cholesterol intake.

If you plan to use the meat on the day of purchase, store it immediately in the original market wrapper in the coldest part of your refrigerator. Meat that will be stored longer should be loosely wrapped in heavy waxed butcher paper and placed in a shallow container or on a plate to catch any drippings. Avoid wrapping meat tightly in plastic film, as it seals in moisture and allows bacteria to grow.

Ground beef and meat cut into small pieces should be used within 2 days of purchase; steaks and roasts within 4 or 5 days. Once cooked, meat to be stored for later use should be covered and refrigerated as soon as it stops steaming; use within 5 days.

If you must freeze beef for later use, quickly rinse it under running cold water and pat dry with paper toweling. Wrap tightly in freezer wrap and seal with freezer tape or seal in freezer bags, pressing out as much air as possible before closing. Ground beef should be cooked within 4 months; other cuts should be used within 6 months for best flavor and texture.

For optimal flavor and texture of thawed meat, remove package from the freezer to a dish placed in the refrigerator and let stand undisturbed until thawed. If you must hurry, thaw in a microwave oven according to the manufacturer's directions.

Buying Beef

By law, all beef sold in the United States must be inspected to insure its wholesomeness before it can be shipped to local markets. Grading of beef, however, is an optional practice that is paid for by wholesale packers who purchase the service from the U.S. Department of Agriculture (USDA). Even though the beef industry is gradually switching to the raising of leaner cattle, the USDA still grades beef according to the amount of fat streaks, or marbling, found in the meat. To some extent, how heavily marbled a piece of meat is reflects how tender and flavorful it is.

The fattiest beef is graded Prime and is produced only in small quantities today, destined primarily for the upscale restaurant trade. It is followed by two considerably leaner grades, Choice and Select (the latter was known as Good until recently). The difference in the fat content of these two grades is quite small, although the Select label is reserved for the least-fatty beef. In Canada, the order of grading has been reversed, with the leanest beef getting the highest rank, a practice many hope to see adopted on this side of the border.

Since the vast majority of us buy our beef from the butcher's display of trimmed meats or in neat little packages, I've chosen not to include the usual diagrammed cow showing where various cuts originate. Most of us prefer not to have such a close identity with the slaughterhouse anyway. Good butchering handbooks are available for those who want to cut up beef at home.

The section known as round, located near the rear end of beef cattle, produces the leanest meat. Careful trimming also transforms cuts from the loin and rib sections, located on the upper center portion of the body, into lean fare. These include the tenderest and most costly cuts of beef: tenderloin, top loin, rib eye. Close paring away of fat turns even inexpensive chuck, taken from up front, into fairly lean cuts.

Fortunately for consumers, federal law now requires that any beef product claiming to be low in fat must print the percentage of fat on the label. To be called "lean," the meat must contain no more than 10 percent fat, while "extra lean" limits the fat to 5 percent.

The law also governs supermarket labels that read "ground beef" or "hamburger." The meat must be only from skeletal muscles (no variety meats) and contain no more than 30 percent fat. To be labeled "ground round" or "ground sirloin," the meat must come entirely from those cuts that do not exceed of 30 percent fat. For the least fatty ground meat, purchase a whole piece of round or other tender lean cut and then have the butcher trim it of all fat and grind it for you. Or take it home, trim it yourself, and then chop it in a food processor or, for a lighter texture, by hand with a sharp knife.

Beef labeled "aged" has been hung for 10 days to 6 weeks in specialized environments with controlled temperature and humidity. During this time excess moisture evaporates, excess blood is drained off, and enzymes partially break down meat fibers to produce more tender beef, which some people also find more flavorful. Although aged beef costs more than nonaged, it goes a bit further because less shrinkage occurs during cooking.

When shopping, make the meat counter the last stop to keep beef as cold as possible while transporting it home. If you'll be delayed or have a long way to travel, place the meat in an ice chest in the car. Select beef that is consistently firm and finely textured all over, blemish free, has no off-odors, and is bright red (plastic-wrapped meat turns dark, but returns to a brighter hue when exposed to the air).

Although the beef industry is attempting to apply uniform common names to beef cuts throughout the nation, local customs often dictate otherwise. For example, strip steaks cut from the top loin may be called "New York" in the Midwest and "Kansas City" in New York; the same steak can also be labeled "Delmonico," "club," or simply "strip." Or a thick cut of choice round called "London broil" in one market may be identified simply as "top round" in another; others know flank as "London broil." Your best bet for demystifying meat nomenclature is to find a butcher whom you can trust and whom you can ask for advice on what cut is best for the dish you are cooking.

In general, for every trimmed and cooked 3-ounce serving, you need to purchase 4 ounces of boneless beef, 4 to 8 ounces of bone-in cuts, and up to 1 pound of very bony meat such as ribs or shank.

PREPARING BEEF FOR COOKING

Beef should be at room temperature before cooking. Use a sharp knife to trim off as much fat as possible. Just before cooking, quickly rinse the meat under running cold water, then pat dry with paper toweling. Before preparing other foods, be sure to wash thoroughly in soapy water and rinse well all cutting boards, knives, dishes, hands, and any other surfaces that were in contact with raw beef.

RAW

Tender cuts of raw beef can be a delight to the palate. The recipes that follow are variations on two classic ways of serving uncooked beef: minced tartare and thinly sliced *carpaccio*. For success, the beef must be of the very best quality.

Western Steak Tartare

1 pound top-quality boneless beef
   tenderloin, sirloin, or top round,
   trimmed of all fat and connective
   tissue and finely ground
¼ cup minced green onion,
   including green tops
¼ cup fresh red or green mild to hot
   chili peppers, stemmed, seeded,
   and minced
1 small fresh prickly pear cactus pad
   (*nopale*), carefully scraped to
   remove any thorns, sliced into
   small pieces, and boiled until
   tender, then well rinsed to
   remove slippery juices, or ¼ cup
   drained canned sliced cactus pad
¼ cup finely chopped red sweet
   pepper
¼ cup finely chopped carrot
¼ cup minced daikon or other
   radish
¼ cup minced fresh cilantro
   (coriander)
¼ cup minced or pressed garlic
Soy sauce, preferably *tamari*
Asian-style sesame oil
Hot chili oil
6 to 10 quail egg yolks in shells
   (optional)
Lime wedges
Salt
Freshly ground black pepper
About 6 buttered whole-grain toast
   slices, cut diagonally into
   triangles

The traditional accompaniments to steak tartare—capers, onion, egg yolk, parsley—have been replaced here by West Coast and Southwest ingredients that reflect Asian and Hispanic influences.

To make bite-sized portions that can be passed on a tray, mix the meat with the other ingredients to taste and spoon onto small toasts, cucumber slices, or into hollowed-out cherry tomatoes or mushrooms.

Mound the beef on a serving platter or form it into a fanciful shape. Arrange the other ingredients around the beef. Diners help themselves to beef and condiments, then mix them all together with 2 forks on individual plates. Spread on toast to eat.

Serves 10 as a starter, or 6 as a main course.

Sliced Raw Beef Appetizers

1 slender French baguette,
    thinly sliced
¼ pound (1 stick) unsalted butter,
    melted
2 pounds top-quality boneless beef
    tenderloin, sirloin, or top round,
    trimmed of all fat and connective
    tissue

MUSTARD SAUCE
1 cup mayonnaise
1 tablespoon Worcestershire sauce,
    or to taste
1 tablespoon Dijon-style mustard
½ teaspoon Tabasco sauce, or to taste
2 tablespoons homemade beef stock
    or canned beef broth
2 teaspoons freshly squeezed lemon
    juice
Freshly ground black pepper
Fresh herbs such as chives, flat-leaf
    parsley, marjoram, or basil for
    garnish

Though usually served as a sit-down first course, this time Italian *carpaccio* has been transformed into an appetizer for passing. For the photograph, I've formed the beef slices into rosettes, placed them in tiny commercially baked pastry cups, and crowned each with a dollop of the mustard sauce and herb garnish. The presentation is also quite festive when made with the buttery toasts described in the recipe.

Preheat an oven to 250° F.

Dip the bread slices in the melted butter, arrange on a baking sheet, and bake until golden brown and crisp, about 30 minutes. Remove from the oven and cool. (Toasts may be made in advance and stored in an airtight container for up to 4 days.)

Quickly rinse the beef under running cold water and pat dry with paper toweling. Wrap in freezer wrap or plastic film and place in the freezer until the meat is very cold but not frozen through, about 2 hours.

To make the sauce, combine the mayonnaise, Worcestershire, mustard, Tabasco, stock or broth, and lemon juice in a small bowl; blend with a wire whisk or a wooden spoon until smooth. Reserve. (Do not make in a blender or food processor; it will be too thin.)

Using an electric slicer or very sharp knife, slice the beef across the grain as thinly as possible. Spread some of the mustard sauce on each piece of toast. Top with the sliced beef, sprinkle with pepper to taste, and garnish with herbs. Arrange on a tray for passing.

Serves 10 to 12 as a starter.

Hot Raw Beef with Fresh Arugula

My partner Lin Cotton recently returned from biking in northern Italy with fond memories of this unusual appetizer. The bottoms of the thin beef slices brown in hot butter on a sizzling plate while the tops stay brilliantly red, combining the succulence of Venetian raw beef *carpaccio* with the buttery richness of just-cooked beef.

Quickly rinse the beef under running cold water and pat dry with paper toweling. Wrap in freezer wrap or plastic film and place in the freezer until very cold but not frozen through, about 2 hours.

Preheat an oven to 450° F.

Using an electric slicer or very sharp knife, slice the beef across the grain about ⅛ inch thick.

Place 1 tablespoon of the butter on each of 4 ovenproof dinner plates. Transfer to the preheated oven until the plates are piping hot and the butter melts but does not brown. Carefully remove the plates from the oven and quickly arrange the beef slices in the center of each plate in a design that simulates the petals on a flower. If using figs, cut partially through into segments, spread apart, and place in the center of beef. Sprinkle with the chopped arugula and pepper to taste and serve immediately.

Serves 4 as a first course.

¾ pound top-quality boneless beef tenderloin, sirloin, or top round, trimmed of all fat and connective tissue
4 tablespoons (½ stick) unsalted butter
4 ripe figs (optional)
½ cup chopped fresh arugula
Freshly ground black pepper

GRILLED & BROILED

The smoky flavor of beef prepared on an outdoor grill simply can not be beat. If the weather or your schedule won't permit backyard cooking, however, any of the outdoor recipes can be adapted to an indoor grill or the broiler.

Only the most tender beef cuts should be trusted to hot coals or a broiler. The meat can be marinated, if desired, for a couple of hours at room temperature, or in the refrigerator for as long as overnight. Marinating adds flavor and helps tenderize the meat.

To prevent the meat from sticking to a grill or broiler rack, the metal surface must be very hot before putting the beef on it. The brief initial contact with the hot surface brands the meat with distinctive grill marks and forms a brown crust that is vital to the marvelous flavor we associate with grilled meat. After searing on each side, the meat can be moved to an area of less intense heat on the grill, or the thermostat on the broiler can be adjusted slightly lower. Be sure to read the manufacturer's directions for your particular type of cooker.

Beef should always be turned with tongs to prevent piercing the meat and allowing precious juices to escape; never use a fork.

The time required to reach the desired degree of doneness varies greatly with the type of grill or broiler, the distance of the meat from the heat source, the position of the meat in relation to direct heat, the thickness of the meat, and the temperature of the meat at the time it goes on the grill. The same techniques described on pages 42 and 43 for judging doneness of roasted meat can be used when grilling. Keep in mind that beef will continue to cook after removing it from the intense heat of a grill or broiler. Therefore, as a general rule it is best to take the meat off a few minutes before you would consider it done, or when the temperature reaches about five degrees less than the guide on the meat thermometer dial.

Cocktail Patty Melts

1 tablespoon unsalted butter
¾ cup thinly sliced yellow onion
1 pound ground sirloin, round, or
    other lean tender beef
2 teaspoons Worcestershire sauce,
    or to taste
Salt
Freshly ground black pepper
4 ounces high-quality Cheddar cheese
8 or more thin slices rye bread
American-style mustard
Sliced cherry tomatoes
Fresh parsley leaflets, preferably
    flat-leaf type

One of Los Angeles's finest contributions to American cooking is the patty melt, a sandwich I've adapted to appetizer-sized portions.

Heat the butter in a sauté pan or skillet over medium heat. Add the onion, cover, reduce the heat to low, and cook for 15 minutes. Remove the cover and cook the onions until very soft and golden, about 45 minutes. Remove from the heat and keep warm.

Prepare a hot charcoal fire or preheat a broiler.

In a bowl, combine the beef, Worcestershire sauce, and salt and pepper to taste. Divide into 16 equal portions. Slice the cheese about ⅛ inch thick, then cut it into 16 squares. Form each portion of meat into a flat patty about ⅛ inch thick and place a piece of cheese in the center. Bring the edges of the meat up and over to cover the cheese and pat the meat into a square, with the cheese encased in the middle of the patty. Grill or broil the burgers until the cheese melts and the meat is done to your preference.

Meanwhile, cut the bread into 16 squares about the same size as the patties. Lightly toast the bread and spread with mustard to taste. Top each bread slice with a meat patty and a dollop of the warm cooked onion. Garnish each with a tomato slice and parsley leaflet.

Serves 6 to 8 as a starter.

Sweet and Tangy Beef Salad

For a fanciful presentation, serve in crisp "rice cups" prepared by frying rounds of edible rice paper in hot oil until golden.

To prepare the fried walnuts, place 3 cups water in a large saucepan over high heat and bring to a boil. Add the walnuts, return to a boil, and cook for 1 minute. Drain the walnuts, rinse under running warm water, and drain again. Transfer the warm nuts to a bowl, pour the sugar over, and stir until the sugar is dissolved.

Pour oil to a depth of 1 inch in a saucepan and heat over medium heat to 350° F., or until a small cube of bread browns quickly when dropped into the oil. Using a slotted spoon, transfer the nuts to the oil and cook, stirring frequently, until golden, about 5 minutes. Remove the nuts to a colander set over a bowl or in the sink and season to taste with salt. Lightly stir for about 5 minutes to keep the nuts from sticking together. Pour onto paper toweling to cool completely. (The fried nuts may be stored in a tightly covered container for up to 2 weeks.)

Prepare a hot charcoal fire or preheat a broiler.

To make the salad, quickly rinse the beef under running cold water and pat dry with paper toweling. Grill or broil the beef until a meat thermometer inserted into the meat registers done to your preference, about 10 minutes per side for medium-rare. Remove from the heat, cool slightly, then slice with the grain into thin strips; reserve.

To make the dressing, combine the safflower oil, sesame oil, chili oil, soy sauce, vinegar, lemon juice, cilantro, ginger, orange zest, and garlic in a bowl and whisk to blend well. Add the beef strips and let stand for about 15 minutes.

Just before serving, remove the beef strips from the dressing with a slotted utensil, reserving dressing. Combine the beef, carrot, red pepper, onion, watercress, mint, and spinach in a large bowl. Add reserved dressing to taste and toss to coat all ingredients. Arrange on a platter or individual plates. Sprinkle with the fried walnuts and serve immediately.

Serves 6 to 8 as a salad course, or 4 as a main course.

FRIED WALNUTS
1 cup walnut halves
2 tablespoons granulated sugar
Safflower or other high-quality vegetable oil for frying
Salt

SALAD
1 pound tenderloin or other tender boneless lean beef, in a single piece about 2 inches thick
¼ cup safflower or other high-quality vegetable oil
2 tablespoons Asian-style sesame oil
1 teaspoon hot chili oil, or to taste
2 tablespoons soy sauce
2 tablespoons rice vinegar
1 tablespoon freshly squeezed lemon juice
2 tablespoons minced fresh cilantro (coriander)
1 tablespoon peeled and minced fresh ginger root
2 teaspoons minced or grated orange zest
1 teaspoon minced or pressed garlic
1 carrot, scraped and cut into julienne or shredded
1 red sweet pepper, stems, membrane, and seeds discarded and cut into very thin julienne
½ red onion, cut in half, thinly sliced, and half-rings separated
2 cups fresh watercress sprigs
1 cup fresh mint sprigs
1 bunch fresh spinach, washed, trimmed and chilled

Corn-Stuffed Steak

MARINADE
¾ cup dry red wine
2 tablespoons olive oil
1 tablespoon Dijon-style mustard
1 tablespoon minced fresh oregano,
    or 1 teaspoon crumbled dried
    oregano
1 teaspoon minced or pressed garlic
Salt
Freshly ground black pepper

2 pounds boneless beef sirloin or
    top round, in a single piece
    about 2 inches thick

STUFFING
2 tablespoons unsalted butter
½ cup finely chopped yellow onion
¼ cup finely chopped red sweet
    pepper
2 tablespoons minced fresh green
    hot chili pepper
½ cup freshly cut corn kernels
¾ cup crumbled corn bread,
    prepared according to your
    favorite recipe
½ cup freshly grated sharp
    Cheddar cheese
1 tablespoon minced fresh cilantro
    (coriander) or parsley, preferably
    flat-leaf type
Salt
Freshly ground black pepper
Ground cayenne pepper

To make the marinade, combine the wine, olive oil, mustard, oregano, garlic, and salt and pepper to taste in a bowl and blend well. Reserve.

Quickly rinse the beef under running cold water and pat dry with paper toweling. Cut a horizontal pocket in the center of one side of the steak, cutting as deeply and as long as possible without piercing the other side or the ends. Place the steak in a flat, shallow nonreactive dish, pour the marinade over, and turn the steak to coat all sides and inside the pocket. Let stand at room temperature for 1 hour, or cover and refrigerate for as long as overnight; bring to room temperature before stuffing.

To make the stuffing, heat the butter in a sauté pan or skillet over medium-high heat. Add the onion and sweet pepper and sauté until soft but not browned, about 5 minutes. Stir in the chili pepper and corn and sauté about 3 minutes longer. Transfer to a bowl. Stir in the crumbled corn bread, grated cheese, minced cilantro or parsley, and salt and peppers to taste.

Prepare a moderate charcoal fire or preheat a broiler.

Remove the steak from the marinade and pat dry with paper toweling; reserve the marinade. Stuff the pocket with the corn bread mixture and close with wooden skewers or sew tightly with cotton thread. Sprinkle the steak with salt and pepper to taste.

Position the hot coals around a pan in the grill to catch drippings and place the steak on the rack over the pan. Cook on each side until done to your preference, about 10 minutes per side for medium-rare, basting occasionally with the reserved marinade.

Let the steak stand about 15 minutes. Discard the skewers or thread and cut the steak into slices about ½ inch thick. Arrange slices on individual plates or a serving platter, spoon pan juices over the slices, and serve warm or at room temperature.

Serves 8.

Grilled Steak Fajitas

MARINADE
¼ cup olive oil, preferably
  extra-virgin
¼ cup freshly squeezed lime or
  lemon juice
¼ cup chopped fresh cilantro
  (coriander)
2 tablespoons chopped fresh oregano,
  or 2 teaspoons crumbled dried
  oregano
1 tablespoon minced shallot or
  red onion
2 teaspoons minced or pressed garlic
1 tablespoon chili powder, preferably
  from *ancho* or *pasilla* peppers
1 teaspoon ground cumin
Salt
Freshly ground black pepper
Ground cayenne pepper

1½ pounds top round or other tender
  boneless lean beef, in 1 or 2 pieces,
  trimmed of all fat and connective
  tissue
2 medium-sized red, green, or gold
  sweet peppers, stems, seeds, and
  membranes removed, sliced into
  ¼-inch strips
1 large yellow onion, sliced vertically
  into ¼-inch strips
12 flour tortillas
About 4 tablespoons (½ stick)
  unsalted butter, melted

Strips of marinated steak hot off the grill are wrapped in warmed flour tortillas for these soft tacos that are now a national rage. In Spanish, *fajitas* means "little belts," an allusion to the skirt steak, cut from the cow's midsection, that was originally used for the dish. Leaner cuts also produce tasty fajitas.

Brush sweet pepper strips and onion slices with oil and grill them alongside the steak strips, then toss the meat and vegetables together before serving. Let diners top off their own fajitas by choosing from a variety of toppings offered in small bowls—grated Jack cheese, chopped red onion, chopped ripe tomato, chopped cilantro, shredded lettuce, and your favorite salsa.

To make the marinade, combine the olive oil, lemon or lime juice, cilantro, oregano, shallot or onion, garlic, chili powder, cumin, and salt and peppers to taste in a bowl and blend well.

Quickly rinse the beef under running cold water and pat dry with paper toweling. Place in a shallow, flat nonreactive container and pour the marinade over the top. Turn the beef in the marinade to coat all sides. Let stand at room temperature for 1 hour or, preferably, cover and refrigerate overnight. Return to room temperature before cooking.

Prepare a hot charcoal fire or preheat a broiler.

Grill or broil the steak until a meat thermometer inserted into the meat registers done to your preference.

Brush the tortillas on one side with melted butter. Wrap in foil and heat over the charcoal or in a preheated 325° F. oven until warm, about 10 minutes. Or place them on a microwave-safe dish, cover with plastic film, and heat at 50 percent power until warm, about 35 to 45 seconds.

Slice the steak with the grain into thin strips and distribute in the center of each warmed tortilla.

Serves 6.

Grilled Steak with Peanut Sauce

Delicious served with fluffy rice cooked in coconut milk and sprinkled with toasted freshly shredded coconut.

To make the marinade, combine the soy sauce, lime juice, peanut butter, brown sugar, curry powder, garlic, and crushed red pepper to taste in a bowl and blend well. Reserve.

Quickly rinse the beef under running cold water and pat dry with paper toweling. Place it in a flat, shallow nonreactive dish, pour the marinade over, and turn the meat to coat well on all sides. Cover with plastic wrap and let stand at room temperature for 2 hours or, preferably, in the refrigerator for as long as overnight. Return to room temperature before cooking.

To make the sauce, combine the peanut butter, coconut milk, lime juice, soy sauce, brown sugar or molasses, ginger, garlic, and cayenne pepper to taste in a saucepan over medium heat and cook, stirring constantly, until the sauce is as thick as heavy cream, about 15 minutes. Transfer to a food processor or blender and purée briefly. Add the beef stock or broth and cream; blend until smooth. Return to the saucepan and heat briefly before serving. (The sauce can be made several hours ahead and refrigerated. Gently reheat before serving.)

Prepare a hot charcoal fire or preheat a broiler.

Cook the steak, turning once and basting with the marinade, until a meat thermometer inserted in the center tests done to your preference. Remove to a cutting surface and thinly slice across the grain at a 45-degree angle. Serve with the warmed peanut sauce.

Serves 8.

MARINADE
½ cup soy sauce, preferably *tamari*
½ cup freshly squeezed lime juice
2 tablespoons crunchy peanut butter
1 tablespoon brown sugar
1 tablespoon curry powder
1 teaspoon minced or pressed garlic
Crushed dried red pepper

2 pounds flank steak, top round, or other tender boneless lean beef, in a single piece, trimmed of all fat and connective tissue

PEANUT SAUCE
⅔ cup crunchy peanut butter
1½ cups unsweetened canned coconut milk
¼ cup freshly squeezed lime juice
2 tablespoons soy sauce
2 tablespoons brown sugar or molasses
1 teaspoon peeled and grated fresh ginger root
2 teaspoons minced or pressed garlic
Ground cayenne pepper
¼ cup homemade beef stock or canned beef broth
¼ cup heavy cream

Korean Barbecued Beef

One of my favorite places to eat in San Francisco is a Korean barbecue house where smoky charcoal grills are brought to the table for cooking paper-thin marinated meats. To save your dining room walls, cook this East Asian classic on the outdoor grill or under the broiler.

The cooked meat is wrapped in lettuce along with condiments selected from an array of choices: *kim chee* (pickled cabbage, available in Asian groceries and some supermarkets), shredded *daikon* (white radish), minced fresh hot chili pepper, raw garlic slices, fresh bean sprouts, shredded carrot, minced green onion, toasted sesame seeds, and hot chili sauce or hot bean paste.

Quickly rinse the beef under running cold water and pat dry with paper toweling. To facilitate slicing, wrap the meat in freezer wrap or plastic film and place in the freezer until very cold but not frozen through, about 2 hours. Cutting diagonally across the grain, slice the meat as thinly as possible.

In a bowl, combine the soy sauce, sugar, sesame oil, garlic, onions, ginger, and pepper to taste and mix well. Add the beef slices, turning to coat well, cover with plastic wrap, and let stand at room temperature, stirring occasionally, for 2 hours, or, preferably, in the refrigerator for as long as overnight. Return to room temperature before cooking.

Prepare a hot charcoal fire or preheat a broiler.

Arrange a plate of chilled lettuce leaves and small bowls of several condiments on the table.

Grill or broil the meat, turning once, for about 30 seconds per side.

To eat, place some of the hot meat on a lettuce leaf, top with selected condiments, wrap the leaf around the meat, and eat out of hand.

Serves 4.

1 pound tenderloin, sirloin, or
    other tender boneless lean beef,
    trimmed of all fat and connective
    tissue

MARINADE
1 cup soy sauce
½ cup granulated sugar
¼ cup Asian-style sesame oil
2 teaspoons minced or pressed garlic
5 or 6 green onions, finely chopped
1 1-inch piece fresh ginger root,
    peeled and minced
Freshly ground black pepper

About 24 lettuce leaves, washed,
    dried, and chilled to crisp
Condiments, see recipe introduction

Middle Eastern Kabobs

MARINADE
4 tablespoons (½ stick) unsalted
    butter, melted
1 teaspoon ground cumin
1 teaspoon ground ginger
½ teaspoon powdered saffron
¼ teaspoon ground cloves
Salt
Ground cayenne pepper
1 cup grated yellow onion
1 tablespoon minced or pressed garlic
¼ cup fresh or canned pomegranate
    juice

2 pounds round, sirloin, or other
    tender boneless lean beef,
    trimmed of all fat and connective
    tissue
16 peeled boiling onions, or 2 small
    white onions, cut into wedges

Countless versions of grilled skewered meat exist throughout the Middle East and have been adapted to local ingredients and seasonings around the world. This one is inspired by the Moroccan kitchen.

During the autumn when fresh pomegranates are in season, cut them in half, squeeze to release juices, and strain out seeds. Freeze for later use. If you can't find fresh pomegranates or bottled juice, substitute red-wine vinegar.

For variety, add other vegetables such as tomato wedges or eggplant slices to the skewers along with the onions.

To make the marinade, combine the butter, cumin, ginger, saffron, cloves, and salt and cayenne pepper to taste in a bowl and blend well. Stir in the onion, garlic, and pomegranate juice. Reserve.

Quickly rinse the beef under running cold water and pat dry with paper toweling. Cut into 1½-inch cubes and place in a flat, shallow nonreactive container. Pour the marinade over, turn the meat to coat well on all sides, and cover with plastic film. Let stand at room temperature for up to 2 hours, or, preferably, in the refrigerator for as long as overnight, turning the beef in the marinade several times. Return to room temperature before cooking.

Prepare a hot charcoal fire or preheat a broiler.

Remove the meat from the marinade, reserving the marinade, and thread it onto metal skewers, alternating with the onion. Cook over the coals or under the broiler, turning several times and brushing frequently with the marinade, until done to your liking, about 12 minutes total cooking time for medium-rare. Use a fork to slide the meat and vegetables off the skewers onto individual plates.

Serves 8.

Garlic Steak Sandwich with Cilantro Salsa

A pungent garlic marinade permeates beef with flavor at the same time that it tenderizes it. The zesty salsa is best served right after it's made, but can be tightly covered and refrigerated for several days.

To make the marinade, combine the wine, lime or lemon juice, garlic, sugar, and salt and cayenne pepper to taste in a bowl and blend well. Reserve.

Quickly rinse the beef under running cold water and pat dry with paper toweling. Place it in a flat, shallow nonreactive dish, pour the marinade over, and turn to coat meat well on all sides. Cover with plastic film and let stand for 2 hours at room temperature, or, preferably, in the refrigerator for as long as overnight. Return to room temperature before cooking.

To make the salsa, chop the garlic in a food processor or blender. Add the cilantro, chili peppers, olive oil, lime or lemon juice, cumin, and salt to taste. Blend until fairly smooth. Reserve.

Prepare a hot charcoal fire or preheat a broiler.

Cook the steak, turning once and basting with the marinade, until a meat thermometer inserted in the center tests done to your preference. Remove to a cutting surface and thinly slice across the grain at a 45-degree angle. Spread the toast with the garlic mayonnaise, if desired. Pile beef slices on toast and generously drizzle with the salsa. Top with onion and tomato, if desired.

Serves 4.

GARLIC MARINADE
½ cup dry red wine
2 tablespoons freshly squeezed
    lime or lemon juice
2 tablespoons minced or pressed garlic
2 tablespoons brown sugar
Salt
Ground cayenne pepper

1 pound flank steak, top round,
    or other tender boneless lean
    beef, trimmed of all fat and
    connective tissue

CILANTRO SALSA
8 to 10 garlic cloves
1¼ cups coarsely chopped fresh
    cilantro (coriander)
6 fresh jalapeño or other green hot
    chili peppers, stemmed and
    seeded, if desired
2 tablespoons olive oil, preferably
    extra-virgin
1 tablespoon freshly squeezed lime
    or lemon juice
1 teaspoon ground cumin
Salt

8 slices sourdough or French bread,
    lightly toasted
Garlic mayonnaise (optional)
Thinly sliced red onion (optional)
Sliced ripe tomato (optional)

Spicy Ground Beef Patties

Seasoned ground beef formed into patties or balls is known by several names—*kofta, kefta, kufta*—in the Middle East. Cooking methods vary as well. The meat may be braised in a thick sauce until tender, panfried, broiled, or baked until golden brown; there is also a version that is served raw. Grilling adds a special flavor.

Serve the patties with fluffy rice, grilled vegetables, and yogurt flavored to taste with grated onion and cucumber, minced mint, and cayenne pepper. To serve as a sandwich, stuff into warmed pita bread pockets, add chopped onion, ripe tomato, and cucumber, and drizzle with the yogurt.

Prepare a moderate charcoal fire or preheat a broiler.

Place the bread in a bowl, add warm water to cover, and let stand until soft, about 4 minutes. Squeeze to press out excess moisture and break into pieces. Transfer to a mixing bowl and add the ground beef, garlic, minced herb, yogurt, curry powder, cumin, cardamom, turmeric, and salt and cayenne pepper to taste. Mix well and form the mixture into about 8 patties each about ½ inch thick.

Grill or broil, turning several times, until brown and done to your taste, about 10 minutes total cooking time for medium-rare. Sprinkle with mint and serve hot.

Serves 4.

2 slices whole-wheat bread
1 pound lean ground beef
1 tablespoon minced or pressed garlic
¼ cup minced fresh cilantro (coriander), mint, or flat-leaf parsley
¼ cup plain low-fat yogurt
2 teaspoons curry powder
1½ teaspoons ground cumin
¼ teaspoon ground cardamom
¼ teaspoon ground turmeric
Salt
Ground cayenne pepper
Minced fresh mint for garnish

Hamburgers

1 pound ground or chopped sirloin,
　　round, or other tender lean beef
Worcestershire sauce (optional)
Unsalted butter (optional)
Salt
Freshly ground black pepper

When I was a child, my daddy would get very frustrated with me when our family went on its weekly outing to dine in one of the best restaurants in nearby Natchez, Mississippi, or Alexandria, Louisiana. He'd most always order a big steak and mother would opt for something unusual she didn't cook at home. But I would always order a plain hamburger, just meat, soft bun, and a generous slather of mayonnaise.

Although my palate has become more adventurous in the decades since, there are still times when all I want is a hamburger. For my birthday dinner just last year, I chose to forgo dining out or having a fancy dinner party in favor of staying home and cooking burgers with my closest friends.

Nowadays, I enjoy my burgers on a lightly toasted French baguette or on a split, lightly toasted whole-grain hamburger bun, topped with grilled or sautéed onion, mayonnaise mixed with garlic, mustard, ripe tomato slices, and sometimes sliced pickle, or, as shown here, with garlic mayonnaise and fresh spinach sautéed in olive oil.

The secret of any good hamburger is full-flavored, tender meat that is freshly chopped by hand with a sharp knife or in the food processor. In either case, the meat should be handled as little as possible. For an occasional change of pace, I add chopped shallot or red onion and Worcestershire sauce to the raw beef. While charcoal grilling is impossible to beat, I frequently follow the panfrying method for steaks described on page 56.

Prepare a hot charcoal fire.

Shape the beef into 4 flat patties about ½ to ¾ inch thick to fit the shape of the bread used. Place on the hot grill and cook until browned on one side. Turn and cook until done to your liking, about 8 minutes total for medium-rare. If desired, sprinkle with Worcestershire sauce and add a small dollop of butter while cooking. Season to taste with salt and pepper.

Serves 4.

ROASTED & BAKED

For some households, special-occasion dinners and holiday feasts traditionally center around a large, magnificent piece of meat, roasted to a perfect turn. In our health-conscious age, such generous portions of red meat are best reserved for these infrequent celebrations.

For year-round dining to serve only a few people, select a small or mini roast about three inches thick from the list of leanest cuts on page 8. Such cuts are at their tender and juicy best when roasted only until the internal temperature registers rare on a meat thermometer (page 43).

For roasting, the piece of beef should be of as even thickness as possible. Reshape uneven meat into a compact and uniform mass, then tie it with cotton string to hold the shape before cooking.

Roasts can be cooked unadorned or with an array of seasonings. I frequently rub roasts with minced garlic and cracked peppercorns before cooking, firmly pressing the garlic and pepper into the surface with the heels of my palms. For variety, spread the raw meat evenly with a glaze of hot pepper jelly, a blend of honey and mustard, chopped chutney, or any other family favorite.

The choice of roasting method is determined by the cut of meat and personal preference. Instead of giving several specific recipes for roasting beef, the next two pages explain three basic methods that you can use or adapt to meet your own needs.

This section also includes recipes for meat loaf, an old-fashioned casserole, and meat pies that are baked in the dry heat of an oven.

High-Heat Roasting

DETERMINING DONENESS BY TOUCH

Some experienced beef cooks rely on touch to determine when the meat is done to their liking. To learn how various cooked stages of meat should feel, press the area between your thumb and index finger on the back of one hand with the index finger of the other hand. When the hand is very relaxed and dangling, this area feels comparable to rare-cooked beef. When the hand is outstretched with tensed fingers, the area has the feel of beef cooked to the medium stage. When the hand is made into a fist, the area mimics the feel of well-done meat. To apply the test to roasting meat, gently poke a lean surface of the beef with a fingertip.

Reserve this method for premium-grade, well-marbled, boneless tender cuts of beef such as tenderloin, eye of round, and rib-eye roasts that are no more than 5 inches thick and do not require long cooking to tenderize the meat. An initial exposure to high heat sears the meat on the outside, then cooks the meat to your liking as quickly as possible. Meat that is to be roasted at high heat should be at room temperature before cooking. This method is not advised for any cut of beef that has been frozen.

For high-heat roasting, preheat an oven to 500° F. Trim as much fat and connective tissue as possible from the roast. Quickly rinse the meat under running cold water and pat dry with paper toweling. For a crispier exterior, place the roast on a wire rack positioned in a shallow roasting pan. Cook until done to your liking, about 7 to 10 minutes per pound for rare or 10 to 15 minutes per pound for medium. If you absolutely must cook meat until it is well done, choose another method of cooking; the exterior will be burned before the internal temperature reaches the well-done stage. Smoking and splattering is normal when roasting at high heat.

Remove the roast from the oven and let it stand for about 15 minutes before carving.

Combined-Heat Roasting

This is the ideal method for cooking tender cuts of bone-in beef or pieces that are thicker than 5 inches. Preheat an oven to 500° F. Trim as much fat and connective tissue as possible from the roast. Quickly rinse the beef in running cold water and pat dry with paper toweling. For a crispier exterior, place the roast on a wire rack positioned in a shallow roasting pan. Cook for 15 minutes. Reduce the heat to 350° F. and continue roasting until the meat is done to your liking; allow a total of 15 minutes per pound plus 15 extra minutes for rare beef, 20 minutes per pound plus an extra 20 minutes for medium, or 25 minutes per pound plus an extra 25 minutes if you absolutely must cook it to the well-done stage.

Remove the roast from the oven and let it stand for about 15 minutes before carving.

Low-Temperature Roasting

The best way to proceed for chuck, rump, or round roast cuts, as well as any beef that is only lightly marbled, is slow cooking. This is also the preferred method for any cut of beef roast that has been frozen and thawed or is cold from the refrigerator, since the exterior does not overcook before the internal temperature has the chance to rise. Low-temperature roasting tenderizes the meat yet keeps it juicy, prevents it from drying out before it is done, and results in evenly colored cooked meat.

Preheat an oven to 350° F. Trim as much fat and connective tissue as possible from the roast. Quickly rinse the meat under running cold water and pat dry with paper toweling. For a crispier exterior, place on a wire rack positioned in a shallow roasting pan and transfer to the oven. Allow 25 minutes per pound plus an extra 25 minutes for rare, 30 minutes per pound plus an extra 30 minutes for medium, and 35 minutes per pound plus an extra 35 minutes if you like well-done meat.

Remove the roast from the oven and let it stand for about 15 minutes before carving.

USING A MEAT THERMOMETER

Since a matter of only a few degrees makes a big difference when cooking meat to your liking, the most reliable way to avoid overcooking beef is to use a meat thermometer.

Insert the thermometer into the thickest part of the beef and leave in place as the meat cooks. Remove the meat from the oven when the internal heat registers done to your liking.

As a general rule, it is best to remove the roast while it is still slightly underdone, as it continues to cook during the resting period before carving.

RARE: internal temperature registers 140° F.; little change in raw color.

MEDIUM-RARE: internal temperature registers around 145° F.; mostly pink throughout.

MEDIUM: internal temperature registers 150° F.; still pink in the center.

MEDIUM-WELL: internal temperature registers around 160° F.; just a trace of pink remains in the center.

WELL DONE: internal temperature registers 165° F.; gray-brown color throughout.

Roast Tenderloin with Assorted Peppercorns

1 beef tenderloin (3 to 4 pounds), trimmed of all fat and connective tissue
1 tablespoon coarse salt
2 tablespoons crushed black peppercorns
2 tablespoons crushed white peppercorns
2 tablespoons crushed green peppercorns
2 tablespoons crushed pink pepperberries
3 tablespoons olive oil, preferably extra-virgin
Assorted whole peppercorns for garnish
Fresh herb sprigs of choice for garnish

In this variation on the preceding basic methods, a beef tenderloin is browned before going into a moderately hot oven. The peppery sliced meat is equally delicious served hot or at room temperature. If serving hot, be sure to collect pan juices or make a simple gravy using beef stock and sautéed wild mushrooms to pass at the table.

Green, black, and white peppercorns are various stages of the same berry from the tropical *Piper nigrum* vine. Green peppercorns are berries that are harvested before ripening and freeze-dried or packed in brine. Black results from drying unripe berries in the sun until their skins turn black, and white are the same dried berries with the skin, or husk, removed. Unrelated pink pepperberries are gathered from the *Schinus molle* tree, a plant to which a few people are allergic.

Quickly rinse the meat under running cold water and pat dry with paper toweling.

Combine the salt and peppers in a small bowl. Rub the mixture all over the beef, pressing the mixture into the meat with the heels of your palms. Let stand at room temperature for 30 minutes, or wrap tightly and refrigerate for up to 2 days; return to room temperature before cooking.

Preheat an oven to 425° F.

In a large sauté pan or skillet over high heat, heat the olive oil almost to the smoking point. Add the beef and brown well on all sides, about 6 to 7 minutes.

Remove from the pan to a well-oiled rack set in a shallow roasting pan. Roast until a meat thermometer inserted in the center registers done to your preference, about 30 to 35 minutes for medium-rare. Remove to a cutting surface and let stand for about 15 minutes.

Carve crosswise into ½-inch-thick slices. Arrange on a serving platter or individual plates, sprinkle with peppercorns, and garnish with fresh herbs.

Serves 12 to 16.

Chuckwagon Meat Loaf

I can never decide whether a good meat loaf is tastier served hot from the oven or cold as a sandwich. Either way, it brings back fond memories of home.

For a crispier crust all around, shape the meat mixture into a mounded round or oblong loaf and cook on a baking sheet or in a shallow pan. Alternatively, pack the mixture into a loaf pan or round ring mold. To form individual servings, as shown, divide the mixture and shape into small loaves or pat it into muffin-tin wells or individual loaf or ring pans and reduce the cooking time; test for doneness as described in the recipe or cook until a meat thermometer inserted in the center registers medium to medium-well (page 43).

In a large mixing bowl, combine the ground beef, sausage, rolled oats or bread crumbs, sesame seeds, yellow or red onion, celery, sweet pepper, green onion, garlic, parsley, oregano, thyme, cumin, horseradish, if using, eggs, ketchup, light cream or half and half, and salt, black pepper, and cayenne pepper to taste. Mix lightly with the tines of two forks or your fingertips to distribute ingredients evenly; avoid overmixing and compacting.

Preheat an oven to 350° F.

Shape the mixture into a mounded round or oblong loaf and place on a lightly greased baking sheet. Bake until the inside is set and the outside feels firm to the touch and is golden brown, about 1 hour; do not overcook. Remove from the oven and let stand about 5 minutes before slicing.

Serves 8.

1½ pounds ground round or other lean tender beef
½ pound hot pork sausage, casing removed and meat crumbled
1 cup rolled oats or unseasoned fine dry bread crumbs, preferably from whole-grain French bread
⅔ cup sesame seeds
2 cups finely chopped yellow or red onion
1 cup finely chopped celery
1 cup finely chopped red or green sweet pepper
½ cup finely chopped green onion, including part of green tops
1 tablespoon minced or pressed garlic
1 cup minced fresh parsley, preferably flat-leaf type
2 tablespoons minced fresh oregano, or 2 teaspoons crumbled dried oregano
1 tablespoon minced fresh thyme, or 1 teaspoon crumbled dried thyme
½ teaspoon ground cumin
2 tablespoons peeled and grated fresh horseradish or prepared horseradish (optional)
2 eggs, lightly beaten
½ cup tomato ketchup
½ cup light cream or half and half
Salt
Freshly ground black pepper
Ground cayenne pepper

Southern Beef and Noodle Casserole

6 ounces dried egg noodles

4 tablespoons (½ stick) unsalted butter

2 tablespoons unbleached all-purpose flour

2 cups milk

Salt

Ground white pepper

1 cup finely chopped yellow onion

¾ cup finely chopped red or green sweet pepper

1 tablespoon minced or pressed garlic

1½ pounds ground round or other lean tender beef

½ pound fresh mushrooms, finely chopped

3 tablespoons top-quality chili powder

Freshly ground black pepper

Ground cayenne pepper

2 cups homemade tomato sauce, or 1 15-ounce can tomato sauce

2 cups homemade creamed corn, or 1 17-ounce can cream-style corn

1 cup (about 3 ounces) freshly grated Cheddar cheese

This is comfort food from my childhood, a dish that my grandmother Olivia Belle Keith cooked back in Jackson, Mississippi. Years later at my fancy-food takeout store in San Francisco, I made my own version of this old-fashioned casserole in huge quantities, since it quickly became a favorite with many customers.

Although Mamaw Keith always made this with flat noodles, fanciful shapes, such as the corkscrew pasta shown here, are more fun.

In a large pot, bring 2 quarts water to a boil over high heat. Add the noodles and cook until *al dente*, about 12 minutes. Drain and rinse in cold water to halt cooking and help keep the strands separated. Reserve.

Melt 2 tablespoons of the butter in a saucepan over medium-high heat. Add the flour, blend well, and cook, stirring, until bubbly, about 1 minute. Slowly whisk in the milk with a wire whisk. Bring to a boil, reduce the heat to medium, and cook, stirring constantly, until thickened, about 5 to 6 minutes. Remove from the heat, season to taste with salt and white pepper, and reserve.

Preheat an oven to 350° F.

Heat the remaining 2 tablespoons butter in a sauté pan or skillet over medium-high heat. Add the onion and sweet pepper and sauté until soft, about 5 minutes. Add the garlic and sauté 1 minute longer. Stir in the ground beef and mushrooms and sauté just until the meat loses its raw meat color, about 5 minutes. Stir in the chili powder. Remove from the heat and season to taste with salt and black and cayenne peppers.

Butter a 2½-quart ovenproof casserole dish. Arrange about half of the noodles in the casserole, cover with about half of the meat mixture, half of the tomato sauce, and half of the corn. Add the remaining noodles, meat, tomato sauce, and corn in the same order. Cover the top with the reserved white sauce and sprinkle with the cheese. Bake until bubbly, about 1 to 1½ hours.

Serves 6.

Corn Pie in Ground Beef Crust
(Pastel de Carne con Elote)

1 tablespoon olive oil
1 cup chopped yellow onion
½ cup chopped celery
½ cup chopped red sweet pepper
2 tablespoons minced fresh hot chili
    pepper
1½ cups peeled, seeded, and chopped
    ripe or canned tomato
1 tablespoon minced or pressed garlic
½ cup golden raisins
1 teaspoon ground cumin
1 tablespoon chili powder, preferably
    from *ancho* or *pasilla* peppers
Salt
Crushed dried red pepper
1 pound ground round or other lean
    tender beef
¼ cup unseasoned fine dry
    whole-wheat bread crumbs
2¾ cups fresh corn kernels,
    from about 4 large ears
1 tablespoon unbleached all-purpose
    flour
2 eggs, lightly beaten
½ cup milk
2 green onions, including green tops,
    thinly sliced
Fresh cilantro (coriander) sprigs

Variations on this casserolelike pie with meat on the bottom and creamy corn pudding on top are found all over Latin America.

Heat the oil in a large sauté pan or skillet over medium-high heat. Add yellow onion, celery, sweet pepper, chili pepper, and tomato and cook, stirring often, until juices have evaporated and vegetables are soft, about 10 minutes. Add garlic, raisins, cumin, chili powder, and salt and dried red pepper to taste; stir and remove from the heat.

Preheat an oven to 350° F.

Combine the ground beef and bread crumbs and add to the vegetable mixture, stirring until well mixed. Spoon into a greased 9-inch square baking dish and smooth the top with the back of a spoon to create an even layer.

Combine the corn, flour, eggs, milk, and green onions and stir to mix well. Pour over the meat layer, spreading evenly. Bake until the center feels set when lightly touched, about 35 minutes. Remove from the oven and let stand for 15 minutes. Cut into squares to serve. Garnish each square with cilantro.

Serves 4 to 6.

Hot Louisiana Meat Pies

FILLING
2 tablespoons lard or solid vegetable
    shortening
¼ cup unbleached all-purpose flour
1½ pounds ground round or other
    lean tender beef
½ pound ground lean pork
2 cups finely chopped yellow onion
6 green onions, including green tops,
    finely chopped
¾ cup finely chopped celery
½ cup finely chopped red or green
    sweet pepper
½ cup chopped fresh parsley,
    preferably flat-leaf type
2 tablespoons minced or pressed garlic
1 tablespoon crushed dried red
    pepper, or to taste
1½ teaspoons ground cayenne
    pepper, or to taste
Salt
Freshly ground black pepper

PASTRY
8 cups unbleached all-purpose flour
4 teaspoons baking powder
1 cup lard or solid vegetable
    shortening, melted and cooled
4 eggs
About 1½ cups milk

1 egg, beaten, for glaze
Ground cayenne pepper for dusting

The town of Natchitoches in northwest Louisiana is justly famed for its spicy meat turnovers. Here's a recipe from my brother-in-law, John Richardson, who attended college there and who is an excellent cook. Be generous with the red pepper; the pies should be fiery.

Although the pies are traditionally deep-fat fried for a few minutes until golden brown, baking reduces the calories and fat. If you're watching cholesterol, choose vegetable shortening instead of the lard called for in the recipe.

To make the filling, melt the lard or shortening in a saucepan over medium-high heat. With a wire whisk or wooden spoon, blend in the flour and cook, stirring, until lightly browned, about 5 minutes. Add the ground beef, pork, yellow and green onion, celery, sweet pepper, parsley, garlic, crushed red pepper, and cayenne pepper and sauté until the meat is browned. Season to taste with salt and peppers. Set aside to cool.

To make the pastry, sift flour and baking powder together into a mixing bowl. Add the melted shortening, eggs, and just enough milk to make a stiff dough. Turn out onto a lightly floured work surface and knead, adding flour a little at a time if necessary, until no longer sticky, about 5 minutes. With a heavy rolling pin, roll dough out as thinly as for pie crust, about ⅛ inch thick. Using a 5½-inch saucer as a guide, cut out about 20 circles with a sharp knife. Roll out each circle as thinly as possible with a few more strokes.

Preheat an oven to 400° F.

Spoon about 3 tablespoons of the filling onto one half of each dough round, moisten the edges of the dough with cold water, fold the other half over the filling, and press edges together. Crimp the edges together with the tines of a fork or a fluted pastry sealer. Arrange the pies on a lightly greased pastry sheet; brush with beaten egg and dust with cayenne pepper. Bake until golden brown, about 15 to 20 minutes. Serve hot or at room temperature.

Makes about 20 pies; serves 10.

Sautéed, Panfried, & Stir-fried

These three methods call for tender cuts of beef that will cook quickly at high heat.

For sautéing or panfrying, select a pan in which the meat fits snugly, but with enough room for the juices to surround it. If it is too crowded, the juices will be trapped underneath the meat and the meat will braise in the liquid rather than cook by direct heat. On the other hand, if there is too much room the juices and fat may burn.

Before adding anything to the pan, place it over high heat and heat it until it is very hot. Then, to add flavor and to prevent the meat from sticking, melt a little butter, heat a little high-quality cooking oil, or rub the bottom with a piece of beef fat. This is especially important when cooking lean beef; fattier beef can usually be cooked in its own fat, which will begin to render as soon as the meat comes in contact with the heat. Add the meat, sear it well in the hot fat, lower the heat, add any other ingredients, and cook until done. After removing the meat, deglaze the pan with wine, stock, or lemon juice, if desired, scraping up any browned bits. Simmer the pan juices until reduced and then pour over the meat as a sauce.

Stir-frying works best in a wok or deep-sided sauté pan. Preheat the pan over high heat, add a little high-quality cooking oil, and swirl to coat the bottom and sides of the pan. When the oil is hot, add the beef, which has usually been tossed with cornstarch and seasonings, to the pan and cook quickly, stirring constantly, until done. To stir-fry vegetables or other additions, remove the beef to a bowl, add more oil, and stir-fry the other ingredients, then return the beef to the pan, add a sauce, if desired, and cook to heat through.

Panfried Steak

About 1 pound tenderloin, sirloin, or other tender boneless lean beef, cut into 4 steaks about 1 inch thick and trimmed of all fat and connective tissue
Freshly ground coarse black pepper
Coarse salt
4 tablespoons (¼ stick) unsalted butter
¼ cup Worcestershire sauce, or to taste
¼ cup minced shallot
¼ cup freshly squeezed lemon juice
1 tablespoon minced fresh parsley, preferably flat-leaf type

For years, this adaptation of *steak au poivre* has been my favorite way of cooking steak. Though any tender beef will work, I most frequently use fillet because I like the texture, and the seasonings impart plenty of flavor to what is a rather bland cut. This method makes a great hamburger as well.

Quickly rinse the steaks under running cold water and pat dry with paper toweling. Generously sprinkle both sides of the steaks with pepper and gently press it into the meat with your hands. Loosely cover with plastic wrap and let stand at room temperature for about 20 minutes.

Place a heavy sauté pan or skillet over high heat and sprinkle a fine layer of salt over the bottom. When the salt begins to brown and the pan is almost but not quite smoking, add the steaks and cook until well browned on the bottom, about 5 minutes for medium-rare. Turn the steak with tongs or two wooden spoons to prevent piercing the steak and releasing juices. Reduce the heat to medium-low. Top each steak with about 1 tablespoon of the butter and sprinkle each with about 1 tablespoon Worcestershire sauce, or to taste. Add the shallots and cook until the steak is done to your preference, about 10 minutes total cooking time for medium-rare. Frequently stir the shallots in the pan drippings, adding a bit more butter and Worcestershire sauce if needed to prevent meat from sticking to the pan.

Remove the steaks to preheated plates; slice, if desired, for an attractive presentation. Add the lemon juice to the pan, scraping the sides and bottom to loosen any browned bits, and cook until reduced, about 1 minute. Remove from the heat, stir in the parsley, and pour over the steaks.

Serves 4.

Sautéed Steak Scallops with Herbed Mustard Sauce

1½ pounds fillet or other tender boneless lean beef, trimmed of all fat and connective tissue
Salt
Freshly ground black pepper
About ¼ pound (1 stick) unsalted butter
¼ cup minced fresh chives
¼ cup minced fresh marjoram, parsley, or thyme, or a combination
1 cup homemade beef stock or canned beef broth blended with 1½ tablespoons cornstarch
1½ tablespoons Dijon-style mustard
1 tablespoon freshly squeezed lemon juice
Worcestershire sauce
About 3 tablespoons Cognac or Madeira, heated
Fresh herb sprigs (same type as minced for garnish)

This variation on steak Diane can be cooked in a chafing dish at the table, but I find it easier to prepare it in the kitchen.

Quickly rinse the beef under running cold water and pat dry with paper toweling. To facilitate slicing, wrap in freezer wrap or plastic film and place in the freezer until very cold but not frozen through, about 2 hours. With an electric slicer or very sharp knife, slice crosswise about ½ inch thick. Place the slices between two sheets of waxed paper and pound with a wooden mallet or flat side of a meat cleaver until very thin. Season to taste with salt and pepper.

In a sauté pan or skillet, heat 2 tablespoons of the butter over medium heat. Add as many of the steaks as will fit comfortably and sauté, turning once, until browned on each side, about 2 minutes total for medium-rare. Remove to a heated platter or individual plates and cook the remaining steaks, adding butter as needed.

When all the steaks are cooked, add 2 tablespoons of the butter to the pan and heat over medium-high heat. Add the chives and minced herb(s) and cook, scraping up any browned bits from the bottom and sides of the pan with a wooden spoon. Stir in the beef stock or broth blended with cornstarch, mustard, lemon juice, and Worcestershire sauce to taste and cook until bubbly. Pour the heated Cognac or Madeira into the pan and ignite it with a long-handled match. When the flames subside, pour the sauce over the steaks, garnish with fresh herb sprigs, and serve immediately.

Serves 6.

Sautéed Tournedos with Fontina and Truffles

To transform this elegant dish into an even more opulent presentation, top with a few thin slices of truffle.

Preheat an oven to 250° F.

Quickly rinse the meat under running cold water and pat dry with paper toweling. Using a saucer or cup as a pattern, trim the meat with a sharp knife to create disks and reserve. Cut the bread slices into the same-sized rounds.

Melt 4 tablespoons of the butter in a sauté pan or skillet over medium heat. Add the bread rounds and sauté, turning several times, until golden brown. Transfer the bread to a baking sheet and continue cooking in the oven until crisp, about 20 minutes. Remove and reserve on the baking sheet.

Preheat a broiler.

In a sauté pan or skillet large enough to hold the beef tournedos without overlapping, heat 2 tablespoons of the remaining butter over medium-high heat. Add the beef and sauté, turning once, until almost done to your preference, about 3 minutes per side for medium rare. Season to taste with salt and pepper and place a tournedos on top of each bread round. Top each piece of beef with a slice of cheese and place under the broiler until the cheese melts, 2 to 3 minutes.

Meanwhile, add the wine to the pan and place over high heat, scraping the pan bottom and sides to loosen any browned bits. Add the stock or broth and reduce to about 2 tablespoons. Remove from heat and stir in the remaining 2 tablespoons butter and the minced truffle, if using, until the butter melts.

To serve, place tournedos on individual serving plates and top each with a few slices of truffle, if using. Spoon some of the sauce over the top and serve immediately.

Serves 6.

6 beef tournedos, cut about 1½ inches thick from small end of tenderloin, trimmed of all fat and connective tissue
6 French bread slices, about ⅜ inch thick
¼ pound (1 stick) unsalted butter
Salt
Freshly ground black pepper
3 ounces Italian Fontina cheese, cut into 6 thin slices to fit tops of beef slices
¼ cup white wine
¼ cup homemade beef stock or canned beef broth
Fresh black or white truffles, thinly sliced, plus some finely minced (optional)

Beef and Wild Mushroom Stroganoff

A Russian classic is updated with the use of wild mushrooms now sold in gourmet markets across the country. When unavailable, use about 4 ounces dried wild mushrooms that have been soaked in warm water to soften; discard tough stems. The more commonplace cultivated mushrooms readily found in supermarkets can also be substituted.

Serve over fluffy rice or buttered fresh noodles made with mushroom, crushed pepper, or other complementary ingredient.

Quickly rinse the beef under running cold water and pat dry with paper toweling. To facilitate slicing, wrap the beef in freezer wrap or plastic film and place in the freezer until very cold but not frozen through, about 2 hours. Using a very sharp knife, slice the beef across the grain into ¼-inch-thick strips, then cut into pieces about 2 inches long. Reserve.

In a saucepan, bring the beef stock or broth to a boil over high heat. Meanwhile, in a separate saucepan, melt 3 tablespoons of the butter over medium-high heat. Stir the flour and ½ teaspoon salt into the butter and beat with a wire whisk until well blended. Cook, stirring, for about 3 minutes. Add the boiling stock or broth all at once and whisk continuously until the sauce is smooth and thickened. Remove from the heat and whisk in the sour cream; reserve.

In a sauté pan or skillet, melt 3 tablespoons of the butter over medium heat. Add the mushrooms and sauté until tender, about 3 to 4 minutes. Season to taste with salt and pepper, transfer to a bowl, and reserve.

In the same pan, heat the remaining 2 tablespoons of butter over medium-high heat. Add the shallot and beef and sauté until beef is golden brown on all sides, about 3 to 5 minutes. Add the reserved sauce, reserved mushrooms, and the sherry, and season to taste with salt and pepper. Heat until warmed through, about 2 or 3 minutes. Do not let it boil or it may curdle. Sprinkle with thyme or parsley and serve immediately.

Serves 6.

1½ pounds fillet, sirloin, or other tender boneless lean beef, trimmed of all fat and connective tissue
1½ cups homemade beef stock or canned beef broth
¼ pound (1 stick) unsalted butter
1½ tablespoons unbleached all-purpose flour
Salt
1 cup sour cream
1 pound fresh wild mushrooms such as *chanterelles*, *morels*, *porcini*, or *shiitakes*, sliced
Freshly ground black pepper
¼ cup minced shallot
3 tablespoons dry sherry, or to taste
Fresh thyme leaves or minced parsley for garnish

Minced Beef with Crisp Greens

Bright ribbons of crisp greens add color and texture to well-seasoned beef when tossed together just before eating.

To prepare the greens for frying, place in a plastic bag or wrap in paper toweling and refrigerate until dry, at least 1 hour or as long as overnight.

Quickly rinse the beef under running cold water and pat dry with paper toweling. Slice into very thin strips, then mince into pieces about the size of the pine nuts. Place in a bowl and sprinkle with 2 tablespoons of the cornstarch and pepper to taste.

In a small bowl, combine the remaining 1 tablespoon cornstarch, the soy sauce, oyster sauce, and sherry and mix well; reserve.

Pour peanut oil in a wok or sauté pan to a depth of about 2 inches and heat to 370° F., or until a piece of the green dropped into the oil sizzles and turns bright green within 10 seconds. Carefully drop the shredded greens into the oil, a handful at a time, and cook until they turn bright green and are crisp, about 10 seconds. Using a slotted spoon, transfer the cooked greens to paper toweling to drain while you cook the beef.

Heat a wok or deep-sided sauté pan over high heat. Add 2 tablespoons of the oil and swirl to coat the bottom and sides of the pan. When the oil is hot, add the beef and stir-fry until lightly browned, about 2 minutes. With a slotted spoon, transfer to a bowl.

Add 1 tablespoon of the oil to the wok or skillet. Add the onion and stir-fry until the green portions are brightly colored, about 30 seconds. Return the beef to the pan. Quickly stir the soy sauce mixture to recombine, add to the pan, and stir-fry until the sauce thickens and everything is heated through, about 1 minute.

Arrange the beef and fried greens in separate mounds on a heated platter and sprinkle the beef with the toasted pine nuts. Toss together at the table.

Serves 4.

1 pound fresh mustard greens
or spinach, stems discarded, leaves
washed in cold water, drained
well, and cut into shreds about
¼ inch wide
1 pound sirloin, flank, or other tender
boneless lean beef, trimmed of all
fat and connective tissue
3 tablespoons cornstarch
Freshly ground black pepper
1 tablespoon soy sauce, preferably
tamari
1 tablespoon oyster sauce
1 teaspoon dry sherry
Peanut or other high-quality
vegetable oil for frying and
stir-frying
½ cup finely chopped green onion,
including green tops
1 cup toasted pine nuts

Thai Beef with Rice Noodles
(Kway Tieow Paht Si-yu)

¾ pound sirloin, flank, or other tender boneless lean beef, trimmed of all fat and connective tissue

1 pound fresh rice noodles, about ¼ inch wide, or ½ pound dried rice noodles, about ¼ inch wide, covered with warm water for five minutes and drained

1 pound fresh spinach, mustard greens, bok choy, or other greens

¼ cup soy sauce, preferably *tamari*

2 tablespoons fish sauce

2 tablespoons molasses or dark brown sugar

Freshly ground black pepper

About ¼ cup peanut or other high-quality vegetable oil

2 tablespoons minced or pressed garlic

2 eggs, beaten

Tiny fresh hot chili peppers or crushed dried red pepper

Rice vinegar or distilled white vinegar for sprinkling

Quickly rinse the beef under running cold water and pat dry with paper toweling. To facilitate slicing, wrap in freezer wrap or plastic film and place in the freezer until very cold but not frozen through, about 2 hours. Using a very sharp knife, slice across the grain as thinly as possible, then slice into strips about 2 inches long and ½ inch wide.

Discard tough stems from the spinach or other greens, wash the leaves thoroughly in cold water, and cut into strips about 1 inch wide.

In a bowl, combine the soy sauce, fish sauce, molasses or brown sugar, and a generous amount of black pepper; stir to blend well and reserve.

Heat a wok or heavy skillet over high heat. When the pan is hot, add 2 tablespoons of the oil, swirl to coat bottom and sides of pan, and heat oil until hot but not smoking. Add the garlic and stir-fry for about 5 seconds. Add the damp shredded greens and stir-fry until brightly colored, about 2 minutes. Transfer to a warmed bowl.

Heat about 2 teaspoons of the oil in the wok or skillet, add the beef, and stir-fry until browned on all sides, about 2 minutes. Transfer to a separate warmed bowl.

Heat about 1 teaspoon of the oil in the cooking pan, add the drained noodles, and toss until heated through, about 2 minutes. Transfer to a warmed bowl.

Heat the remaining 2 teaspoons of the oil in the pan, add the eggs, and cook, without stirring, until they are just set, about 30 seconds. Break up the eggs and stir in the reserved noodles, greens, beef, and fresh chili peppers or dried red pepper to taste. Quickly stir the soy sauce mixture to recombine, add to the pan, and stir-fry until all ingredients are heated through and well coated with the soy mixture. Transfer to a heated platter and serve immediately. Pass the vinegar at the table for sprinkling on top.

Serves 4.

Fiery Orange Beef, Hunan Style

1½ pounds sirloin, flank, or other
    tender boneless lean beef,
    trimmed of all fat and connective
    tissue
2 tablespoons peeled and minced
    fresh ginger root
1 tablespoon granulated sugar
3 tablespoons cornstarch
3 tablespoons Chinese cooking wine
    (*Shaoxing*) or dry sherry
3 tablespoons soy sauce
1 tablespoon rice vinegar
¼ cup homemade beef stock or
    canned beef broth
About 2 tablespoons peanut or other
    high-quality vegetable oil
½ cup dried orange peel, softened
    in hot water for about 5 minutes
    and drained
3 green onions, including green tops,
    thinly sliced
1 teaspoon minced fresh red hot chili
    pepper, or to taste
4 whole fresh or dried small
    red hot chili peppers
Slivered green onion for garnish

Dried orange or tangerine peel, available in Asian markets and many shops that sell herbs, is more potent than fresh. Home-dried peel is even more flavorful. To prepare, thinly peel the zest from several Mandarin oranges or tangerines with a swivel-blade vegetable peeler. With a small knife, slice the zest into long thin strips, arrange them on a baking sheet, and place in a 225° F. oven until dried, about 45 minutes. Store in an airtight container for up to a year.

Quickly rinse the beef under running cold water and pat dry with paper toweling. Cut the meat into strips about 2 inches long and ¼ inch wide and place in a bowl. Sprinkle with the ginger, sugar, 1½ tablespoons of the cornstarch, 1 tablespoon of the wine, and 1 tablespoon of the soy sauce. Mix well to coat the beef and reserve.

In a small bowl, combine the remaining 1½ tablespoons cornstarch, 2 tablespoons wine or sherry, and 2 tablespoons soy sauce, the vinegar, and the beef stock or broth. Stir to blend and reserve.

Heat a wok or deep-sided sauté pan over high heat, add about 1 tablespoon of the oil, and swirl to coat bottom and sides of pan. Add half of the beef and stir fry until browned, about 3 minutes. Remove to a heated bowl. Heat another tablespoon of oil, add the remaining beef, and stir-fry until browned. Transfer to the bowl holding the first batch of beef.

Heat the remaining tablespoon of oil in the pan. Add most of the orange peel (reserve some for garnish), the sliced green onions, and the minced and whole chili peppers and stir-fry until the onions are bright green, about 1 minute. Add the cooked beef and stir to blend. Quickly stir the reserved cornstarch mixture to recombine and stir it into the beef. Cook until the liquid evaporates and the beef is well glazed, about 2 minutes. Garnish with slivered green onion and reserved orange peel and serve immediately.

Serves 6.

BRAISED & SIMMERED

This section begins with a slowly simmered basic beef stock, an ingredient essential to the making of good soups, sauces, and other dishes. Following the stock are a variety of recipes in which beef is braised or simmered in a hot liquid. The cooking medium may be anything from a mixture of ground chili peppers and water, as in Red Chili Beef, New Mexico Style, to the beer in Belgium's traditional *carbonnade de boeuf*.

Most often, the beef is browned first, then the liquid is added and the meat is simmered on the stove top or in an oven until tender.

Beef Stock

3 pounds beef bones
3 pounds beef chuck
2 large yellow onions, quartered
3 celery ribs, cut into 2-inch lengths
3 large carrots, cut into 2-inch pieces
2 cups coarsely chopped leeks,
      including tender green tops
2 large parsnips, cut into 2-inch pieces
2 large turnips, quartered
2 bay leaves
4 or 5 fresh parsley sprigs, preferably
      flat-leaf type
4 or 5 fresh thyme sprigs
1 teaspoon whole black peppercorns
Salt
5 quarts water

A full-flavored stock is vital to the success of many dishes. Make at your convenience and keep refrigerated for up to 5 days, or freeze in small, handy-sized portions.

To serve as a clear consommé or to use in making aspic, clarify the stock as directed in the note at the end of the recipe. I like to add steamed julienned vegetables, as shown, to the consommé before serving.

Combine the beef bones and meat in a large pot, add cold water to cover, and bring to a boil over high heat. Reduce the heat and simmer for 5 or 6 minutes. Drain and discard liquid and rinse the meat and bones under running cold water. Drain again and transfer to a large stockpot.

Add all the remaining ingredients to the stockpot and bring to a boil over medium-high heat. Reduce the heat to low and simmer, partially covered, for 4 to 5 hours. Use a slotted or wire utensil to skim the surface frequently to remove any foam and scum. Remove the cover completely during the last hour of cooking.

Strain through a wire sieve, discard the bones and vegetables, and reserve the meat for another purpose.

Makes about 3 quarts.

NOTE: To clarify the stock for serving as consommé or to use for aspic, combine 5 egg whites and 5 crushed egg shells in a clean stockpot and beat with a wire whisk until the egg whites are frothy. Add the strained stock and place the pan over medium-low heat, stirring constantly, until the mixture comes to a boil. Reduce the heat to low and simmer for 45 minutes. Strain through a colander or sieve lined with 3 layers of dampened cheesecloth.

Siberian Borscht with Meatballs

Aylett Cotton of Hillsborough, California, brought this authentic recipe home from a trip to the Soviet Union.

To make the meatballs, heat the butter in a small skillet over medium-high heat. Add the onion and sauté until soft, about 5 minutes. Add the garlic and sauté 1 minute longer. Transfer to a bowl, stir in the beef, bread crumbs, cheese, egg, and salt and pepper to taste. Form into balls about 1 inch in diameter.

In a deep skillet, bring the stock to a boil over medium-high heat. Add as many meatballs at a time as will fit comfortably in the pan and cook, skimming off foam as necessary, until done, about 15 minutes. Remove meatballs with a slotted spoon and reserve; cook remaining meatballs in the same way. Discard the stock and reserve the meatballs.

To make the borscht, heat 3 tablespoons of the butter in a saucepan over medium-high heat. Add the beets and sauté until well coated with butter, about 2 minutes. Stir in the tomato paste, vinegar (to preserve bright beet color), and 1 quart of the stock or broth. Bring to a boil, cover, reduce the heat to low, and simmer until the beets are tender, about 20 minutes.

In a separate saucepan, cover the potatoes with water and bring to a boil over medium-high heat. Cook until the potatoes are tender but not mushy. Remove from the heat, drain, and let stand until cool enough to handle, then peel and cut into small dice.

Heat the remaining 2 tablespoons of butter in a sauté pan or skillet over medium-high heat. Add the onion and carrot and sauté until tender but not browned, about 5 minutes. Remove from the heat and reserve.

Add the remaining 1 quart soup stock to the beets. Stir in the reserved sautéed onion-carrot mixture and shredded cabbage. Bring to a boil over medium-high heat and cook until the cabbage is tender, about 15 minutes. During the last 5 minutes of cooking, add the reserved potatoes, beans, and meatballs just to heat through. Season to taste with salt and pepper.

Ladle the soup into bowls, add a dollop of sour cream or crème fraîche to each bowl, and sprinkle with dill.

Serves 6.

MEATBALLS
1 tablespoon unsalted butter
¼ cup grated or minced yellow onion
½ teaspoon minced or pressed garlic
½ pound ground lean beef
¼ cup unseasoned fine dry bread crumbs
1 cup shredded mild cheese such as Monterey Jack
1 egg
Salt
Freshly ground black pepper
1 quart homemade beef stock or canned beef broth

BORSCHT
5 tablespoons unsalted butter
1 pound beets, peeled and cut into julienne (about 4 cups)
2 tablespoons tomato paste
2 tablespoons red wine vinegar
2 quarts homemade beef stock or canned beef broth
½ pound boiling potatoes
½ cup chopped yellow onion
½ cup chopped carrot
1 cup white navy beans, soaked overnight in cold water to cover, then cooked in soaking water until tender and drained
4 cups (about 1 pound) shredded cabbage
Salt
Freshly ground black pepper

Sour cream or crème fraîche for garnish
Chopped fresh dill for garnish

Beef Chili, Texas Style
(Chili con Carne)

3 pounds round or other tender
    boneless lean beef, trimmed
    of all fat and connective tissue
3 tablespoons safflower or other
    high-quality vegetable oil
2 cups finely chopped yellow onion
1 tablespoon minced or pressed
    garlic, or to taste
¾ cup ground chili powder,
    preferably freshly ground from
    dried *ancho* or *pasilla* peppers
1 tablespoon ground cumin, or
    to taste
½ cup unbleached all-purpose flour
Salt
Freshly ground black pepper
Ground cayenne pepper
3 cups homemade or canned tomato
    sauce
4 cups cooked dried or canned black
    or pinto beans (optional)

One of America's most popular dishes started out as a campfire stew for hungry cowboys, who laced it with wild chili peppers to give it plenty of kick. Today there are about as many "authentic" recipes for chili as there are cooks in Texas, some swearing by cubed beef instead of ground, some arguing for beans and others against them.

This easy yet tasty version comes from my sister Martha, who wraps it in warm tortillas with an array of toppings as described for Grilled Steak Fajitas (page 26). It is also good served in bowls with the garnishes passed.

Latin groceries sell a number of different chilies already ground to a powder. These products are generally more flavorful than most commercial spice blends labeled as chili powder found on supermarket shelves.

Quickly rinse the beef under running cold water and pat dry with paper toweling. Chop the beef with a sharp knife or in a food processor, or cut it into ½-inch cubes. Reserve.

Heat the oil in a dutch oven or other heavy pot over medium heat. Add the onion and cook until soft, about 5 minutes. Add the beef and garlic and cook until the meat is just past the pink stage. Add the chili powder, cumin, flour, and salt, black pepper, and cayenne pepper to taste; mix well. Stir in the tomato sauce, reduce the heat, and simmer, uncovered, until the flavors are well blended, about 1 hour. Stir in the cooked beans, if using, the last 20 minutes of cooking. Add a little water to the pot anytime during the cooking if the mixture begins to dry out.

Serves 12.

Red Chili Beef, New Mexico Style
(*Carne en Salsa Roja*)

Margie Sandoval Allen, a grand cook who learned to make chili from her mother in Santa Fe, taught me how to make this authentic Southwest dish. Look for long, shiny whole dried red *pasilla* chilies or dark wrinkled *ancho* chilies in Spanish markets.

I enjoy this chili spooned over stacked or rolled cheese-filled enchiladas made with blue-cornmeal tortillas. It is also good served in bowls and accompanied with tortillas, chips, or corn bread made from the blue cornmeal unique to Southwest pueblos.

Preheat an oven to 400° F.

Quickly rinse the beef under running cold water and pat dry with paper toweling. Cut into ½-inch cubes. Reserve.

Discard the stems from the chilies. Split open and remove seeds and membranes, if desired. (That's where much of the heat is stored.) Mist the chilies with water and lay them on a baking sheet. Roast in the oven for about 5 minutes.

Place half of the chilies and about 3 inches of water in a food processor or blender and purée until fairly smooth, adding more water if needed. Transfer to a saucepan. Blend the remaining chilies in the same way. Combine the onion and garlic in the food processor or blender, chop finely, and add to the chilies.

Add the reserved beef to the chili mixture and bring to a boil over medium-high heat. Cover, reduce the heat to low, and simmer, stirring occasionally, until the beef is very tender, about 30 minutes. Season to taste with salt.

Serves 12.

3 pounds round or other tender boneless lean beef, trimmed of all fat and connective tissue
About 12 dried large New Mexican chili peppers
1 cup coarsely chopped onion
6 to 8 garlic cloves, peeled
Salt

Beef Cooked in Broth, Japanese Style (Shabu Shabu)

1½ pounds tenderloin, sirloin, or
    other tender boneless lean beef,
    trimmed of all fat and connective
    tissue

DIPPING SAUCE
½ cup sesame seeds
½ cup soy sauce, preferably *tamari*
3 tablespoons homemade beef stock
    or canned beef broth
2 tablespoons rice wine (*sake*)
2 teaspoons granulated sugar

2 pieces firm soybean curd (*tofu*),
    cut into 1-inch dice
8 green onions, including part of
    the green tops, cut into 3-inch
    lengths, then slivered lengthwise
2 carrots, scraped and cut into
    julienne
½ cup sliced canned bamboo shoot
2 cups fresh or dried Japanese
    wheat noodles (*udon*) or
    buckwheat noodles (*soba*)
About 12 fresh young spinach leaves,
    stemmed
Cooked white rice
5 cups delicately flavored homemade
    beef stock, or 3 cups canned beef
    broth diluted with 2 cups water
1 3- to 4-inch square dried sea kelp
    (*kombu*)

This Japanese version of beef fondue, in which thin slices of beef and vegetables are simmered in hot broth is traditionally cooked at the table. Once the meat and vegetables have been eaten, the broth is served as soup.

Quickly rinse the beef under running cold water and pat dry with paper toweling. To facilitate slicing, wrap the beef in freezer wrap or plastic film and place in the freezer until very cold but not frozen through, about 2 hours. With an electric slicer or a very sharp knife, slice the meat with the grain as thin as possible, then cut each slice in half crosswise.

To make the dipping sauce, place the sesame seeds in a small skillet over medium-high heat and cook, shaking the pan or stirring frequently, until lightly toasted, about 3 minutes. Transfer to a blender or food processor, add the soy sauce, stock or broth, rice wine, and sugar, and blend until smooth. Reserve.

Arrange the beef, soybean curd, green onion, carrot, bamboo shoot, noodles, and spinach on a tray. Divide the dipping sauce among 6 small bowls. Provide each person with chopsticks or a long-handled fork, a bowl of the sauce, a bowl of rice, and a small bowl and spoon for soup.

Combine the stock or broth and the sea kelp in an electric skillet or cooking pot with a portable heat source placed on the dining table. Bring to a boil over high heat, then reduce the heat so that the liquid simmers throughout the cooking.

Each person takes a piece of beef with chopsticks or a fork and swishes it around in the simmering broth until done to his or her preference, about 3 seconds for medium-rare. Then the meat is dipped into the sauce and eaten. The vegetables are cooked in the same way. The rice is an accompaniment.

When all the meat and vegetables have been eaten, add the noodles to the broth and cook until tender, about 6 to 8 minutes. Discard the dried kelp, ladle the broth and noodles into bowls, and eat as a soup.

Serves 6.

Braised Beef Bundles

Thin scallops of beef rolled around a stuffing are known as *paupiettes* to the French, *rollatini* to the Italians, *rouladen* to the Germans, and sometimes as "birds" or "olives" in the English-speaking world. The fillings change with the cuisine, but the preparation and the cooking technique are basically the same. Serve these flavorful "bundles" with pasta, with some of the sauce spooned over the top.

Quickly rinse the beef under running cold water and pat dry with paper toweling. To facilitate slicing, wrap in freezer wrap or plastic film and place in the freezer until very cold but not frozen through, about 2 hours. Thinly slice the meat with a sharp knife into about 16 rectangular pieces. Place each piece between two pieces of waxed paper and lightly pound with a wooden mallet or the flat side of a meat cleaver until very thin.

In a bowl, combine the ham, cheese, walnuts, raisins, mustard, garlic, and salt and pepper to taste and mix thoroughly. Mound a portion of the mixture near one end of each piece of the pounded meat. Roll the meat from the end nearest the stuffing, tucking the edges in as you roll to form a pillow-shaped packet. Tie around the middle and then lengthwise around each roll with cotton string.

In a pan just large enough to hold all of the rolls, heat the oil over medium heat. Add the rolls and brown on all sides, turning frequently. Blend the stock or broth with the tomato paste and add the mixture to a depth of two-thirds up the sides of the beef rolls. Season to taste with salt and pepper. Bring to a boil over medium-high heat, then cover, reduce the heat to very low, and simmer until very tender, about 1½ to 2 hours, frequently basting and turning the rolls. Remove the rolls to a warm plate. Increase the heat to high and cook the sauce until reduced somewhat.

Cut and remove the strings from the rolls before serving. Spoon some of the pan sauce over each bundle.

Serves 8.

2 pounds round, flank, or other tender boneless lean beef, trimmed of all fat and connective tissue
½ pound thinly sliced flavorful baked ham, chopped
½ cup freshly grated Parmesan cheese, preferably Parmigiano-Reggiano
2 tablespoons chopped walnuts
2 tablespoons raisins, soaked in warm water until plumped, then drained
1 teaspoon Dijon-style mustard
1 teaspoon minced or pressed garlic
Salt
Freshly ground black pepper
2 tablespoons olive oil, preferably extra-virgin
About 3 cups homemade beef stock or canned beef broth
3 tablespoons tomato paste

California Ranch Oven Stew

2 pounds boneless lean beef top
    round, trimmed of all fat and
    connective tissue
Garlic pepper (available on many
    supermarket spice shelves)
    or freshly ground black pepper
Salt
2 large yellow onions, sliced
6 garlic cloves, sliced
3 or 4 potatoes, peeled and cut
    into 1-inch cubes
3 carrots, scraped and cut into
    1-inch lengths
3 celery ribs, cut into 1-inch lengths
1 cup thickly sliced mushrooms
2 cups shelled fresh or frozen peas
About 5 cups plain or spicy tomato
    juice

Peter Baumgartner, who grew up on a ranch near San Juan Bautista, gave me the idea for this super easy one-pot meal. All the cooking takes place while you go about your chores. The low temperature keeps the vegetables from overcooking and falling apart during the lengthy oven stint.

Preheat an oven to 300° F.

Quickly rinse the beef under running cold water and pat dry with paper toweling. Cut into 1-inch cubes and season to taste with garlic pepper and salt. Transfer to a dutch oven or other heavy ovenproof casserole. Add the onions, garlic, potatoes, carrots, celery, mushrooms, and peas. Pour in enough tomato juice to cover the ingredients by about ½ inch. Cover tightly and place in the oven above a baking sheet or large piece of foil set on a lower rack to catch any juices that overflow. Cook until the meat is tender, about 4 to 6 hours.

Serves 8.

South American Spicy Beef Stew (Picadillo)

2 pounds round or other boneless lean beef, trimmed of all fat and connective tissue
Salt
2 tablespoons olive oil, preferably extra-virgin
1 cup finely chopped yellow onion
1 cup finely chopped red or green sweet pepper
2 teaspoons minced or pressed garlic
3 cups peeled, seeded, and chopped ripe or canned tomatoes
⅓ cup small pimiento-stuffed green olives
¼ teaspoon ground cloves
½ teaspoon ground cumin
1 tablespoon red-wine vinegar
¾ cup raisins
½ cup slivered almonds

Back in the days of my Twin Peaks Gourmet in San Francisco, the kitchen turned out vats of this delicious stew for scooping into takeout containers. Serve over fluffy rice, if desired.

Quickly rinse the beef under running cold water and pat dry with paper toweling. Cut into 1-inch cubes.

Place the beef in a dutch oven or heavy fire-resistant casserole. Sprinkle with about 2 teaspoons salt and add just enough water to cover. Bring to a boil over medium-high heat. Cover, reduce heat to low, and simmer until the beef is tender, about 1½ hours. Uncover and simmer until most of the liquid has evaporated, about 1 hour longer.

While the meat cooks, heat the oil in a large sauté pan or skillet over medium-high heat. Add the onion and sauté until soft, about 5 minutes. Add the sweet pepper and sauté until soft, about 5 minutes longer. Add the garlic and sauté 1 minute longer. Stir in the tomatoes, olives, cloves, cumin, and vinegar and bring to a boil. Cover and simmer 15 minutes, then uncover and cook until the sauce is thickened, about 30 minutes.

Transfer the tomato sauce to the pot holding the cooked beef. Stir in the raisins and simmer, stirring frequently, for 10 minutes. Stir in the almonds and heat through.

Serves 8.

Belgian Beef and Beer Stew
(*Carbonnade de Boeuf*)

Serve this Old World recipe with a glass of Belgian beer or ale. Boiled new potatoes and sautéed apple slices are traditional accompaniments.

Quickly rinse the beef under running cold water and pat dry with paper toweling. Cut the meat lengthwise into long strips that are about 2 inches wide by 2 inches high, then slice crosswise about ⅛ inch thick. Reserve.

In a large sauté pan or skillet, cook the bacon over medium heat until crisp. Using a slotted spoon, transfer pieces to paper toweling to drain. Reserve drippings in pan.

Avoiding crowding by working in batches, add the beef to the bacon renderings and cook until well browned on all sides, about 6 minutes per batch. With a slotted spoon, transfer the browned meat to a dutch oven or ovenproof casserole. Continue cooking until all the meat is browned.

Stir the butter into the cooking fat, scraping the bottom and sides to loosen browned bits of beef. Reduce the heat to low, add the onion and sugar, and cook, stirring occasionally, until the onion is almost caramelized, about 25 to 35 minutes. Add the garlic and cook 1 minute longer. Transfer the mixture to the casserole.

Stir into the casserole the reserved bacon, the bay leaves, parsley, thyme, stock or broth, beer or ale, vinegar, and salt and pepper to taste. Bring to a boil over medium-high heat, cover, reduce the heat to low, and simmer, stirring occasionally, until the beef is very tender, about 1½ to 2 hours. If necessary, add a little more stock or beer during cooking to prevent meat from sticking. Alternatively, cook in a preheated 325° F. oven.

Pour the stew through a sieve, collecting the sauce in a saucepan. Arrange the meat on a heated platter. Skim any collected fat off the sauce, then bring it to a boil over high heat. Scatter the sliced cornichons over the meat and pour the hot sauce over the top. Garnish with whole cornichons and sprinkle with thyme leaves or parsley.

Serves 8.

2 pounds round or other boneless lean beef, trimmed of all fat and connective tissue
3 thick strips bacon, cut into ½-inch pieces
2 tablespoons unsalted butter
3 cups thinly sliced yellow onion
1 teaspoon granulated sugar
2 teaspoons minced or pressed garlic
2 bay leaves
2 tablespoons minced fresh parsley, preferably flat-leaf type
1 tablespoon minced fresh thyme, or 1 teaspoon crumbled dried thyme
½ cup homemade beef stock or canned beef broth
1 cup beer or ale, preferably Belgian
2 tablespoons cider vinegar
Salt
Freshly ground black pepper
3 tablespoons sliced cornichons
Whole cornichons for garnish
Fresh thyme leaves or minced parsley for garnish

Sicilian Stuffed Beef Roll
(Farsumagru)

Farsumagru, Sicilian dialect for "false lean," describes the simple and lean appearance of the roll until slicing reveals the riches inside.

Heat 2 tablespoons of the olive oil in a sauté pan or skillet over medium-high heat. Add the onion and sauté until soft but not browned, about 5 minutes. Add the garlic and sauté 1 minute. Add the spinach and sauté until the spinach turns bright green, about 3 minutes. Transfer to a mixing bowl. Stir in the ground beef, Parmesan cheese, bread crumbs, parsley, egg, nutmeg, and salt and pepper to taste.

Quickly rinse the beef under running cold water and pat dry with paper toweling. Lay the meat on a flat surface and use a sharp knife to butterfly it by slicing horizontally, leaving one edge intact. Spread the steak out and gently pound with a wooden mallet or the flat side of a meat cleaver to an even thickness. Layer the mortadella slices on top of the meat, then spread with the spinach mixture. Sprinkle the peas over the spinach. Beginning at one long side, roll the meat up jelly-roll fashion, tucking in ends, and tie securely in several places with cotton string.

Heat the remaining 3 tablespoons of olive oil in a dutch oven or large pot over high heat. Brown the beef roll on all sides. Stir the tomato paste, wine, and stock or broth together in a bowl and pour over the meat. Bring the liquid to a boil. Cover, reduce the heat to low, and simmer until the beef is tender when pierced with a fork, about 1½ to 2 hours, turning several times and adding more stock, broth, or water if necessary to maintain about 1 cup liquid.

Remove the beef to a cutting surface and let stand for about 10 minutes. Meanwhile, place the pan over high heat and reduce the sauce if it seems too thin. Remove the strings and carve the roll into ¼-inch-thick slices. Season the hot pan juices with salt and pepper to taste and spoon over the meat.

Serves 8.

5 tablespoons olive oil, preferably extra-virgin
1 cup chopped yellow onion
1 teaspoon minced or pressed garlic
1 bunch fresh spinach, stems discarded, leaves washed and chopped
4 ounces lean ground beef
¼ cup freshly grated Parmesan cheese, preferably Parmigiano-Reggiano
¼ cup fine dry bread crumbs, preferably from French or Italian bread
3 tablespoons chopped fresh parsley, preferably flat-leaf type
1 egg, lightly beaten
½ teaspoon freshly grated nutmeg
Salt
Freshly ground black pepper
2 pounds boneless top round, in a single piece about ½ inch thick, trimmed of all fat and connective tissue
¼ pound mortadella, sliced ⅛ inch thick
½ cup shelled fresh or thawed frozen green peas
2 tablespoons tomato paste
1 cup dry red wine
1 cup homemade beef stock or canned beef broth

Pot Roast with Root Vegetables

3-pound piece eye of round or other
    boneless lean beef cut, trimmed
    of all fat and connective tissue
3 tablespoons high-quality
    vegetable oil
Salt
Freshly ground black pepper

SEASONING MIXTURE
2 medium-sized yellow onions
2 carrots, cut in half
2 celery ribs, cut in half
2 bay leaves
3 fresh parsley sprigs, preferably
    flat-leaf type
3 fresh thyme sprigs, or 1 teaspoon
    crumbled dried thyme
About 3 cups homemade beef stock,
    canned beef broth, or water

ROOT VEGETABLES
12 small white onions, peeled
12 small carrots, scrubbed and
    trimmed, then scraped if desired
12 small parsnips, scrubbed and
    trimmed, then scraped if desired
12 small new potatoes
12 small turnips or rutabagas, peeled
12 small beets
1 head garlic, peeled and cloves
    separated

About 1 tablespoon unbleached
    all-purpose flour (optional)
Minced fresh herbs of choice
    for garnish

This old-fashioned dish is so succulent it's difficult to restrict yourself to a 3-ounce serving portion.

Preheat an oven to 325° F.

Quickly rinse the beef under running cold water and pat dry with paper toweling. If necessary to form a compact mass, tie with cotton string in several places. Reserve.

Heat the oil in a dutch oven or other heavy casserole over high heat. Add the meat and brown well on all sides. Drain off and discard all but 3 tablespoons of fat and season the meat to taste with salt and pepper. Add the seasoning mixture, including onions, carrots, celery, bay leaves, parsley, thyme, and enough stock, broth, or water to come halfway up the sides of the roast. Bring to a boil over high heat, then cover tightly and transfer to the oven. Cook until the meat is just tender, about 1½ hours, adding a little more liquid to maintain about 2 cups liquid at all times; skim off fat as it accumulates and occasionally baste the meat with the simmering liquid. Remove from the oven and discard the seasoning vegetables.

Arrange the root vegetables, including onions, carrots, parsnips, potatoes, turnips or rutabagas, beets, and garlic in the stock remaining around the roast and sprinkle them with salt and pepper to taste. If necessary, add additional stock, broth, or water to come halfway up the depth of the vegetables. Cover tightly, return to the oven, and cook, basting the roast and vegetables occasionally with the liquid, until the vegetables are just tender and the meat is very tender but not falling apart, about 30 minutes longer.

Remove the roast from the pot and let stand for about 15 minutes. Discard string, if used. Carve the roast (don't expect perfect slices) and arrange on a heated platter. Peel the beets and arrange them with the other vegetables around the beef. If the pan drippings seem too thin, whisk in flour and cook over medium-high heat until the flour loses its raw taste and the gravy is thickened, about 3 minutes. Pour the pan drippings over the meat, sprinkle with herbs, and serve immediately.

Serves 12.

INDEX

Aged beef 9

Braising techniques 71
Broiling techniques 19
Buying beef 8-9

Calories 6
Choice beef 8
Cholesterol 7
Combined-heat roasting 43
Common names for cuts 9
Cooking methods 19, 41-43, 55, 71

Determining doneness 42, 43

Fat 6, 9
Fatty acids 7
Flank steak 7
Freezing beef 8

Grading beef 8
Grilling techniques 19

High-heat roasting 42

Introduction 5

Labels, understanding 8, 9
Leanest cuts 7
Liver 5
Low-temperature roasting 43

Meat thermometer 43
Medium, defined 43
Medium-rare, defined 43
Medium-well, defined 43

Nutrition 6-7

Oelic acid 7

Panfrying techniques 53
Preparing for cooking 9
Prime grade beef 8
Protein 6

Rare, defined 43
Raw beef 11
Roasting techniques 41-43
Round 7, 8

Sautéing techniques 53
Select grade beef 8
Shopping for beef 8-9
Short loin, 7
Simmering techniques 71
Sirloin 7
Stearic acid 7
Stir-frying techniques 53
Storing beef 8

Thawing frozen beef 8
Trimming fat 8

USDA grades 8
Using a meat thermometer 43

Vitamins in beef 7

Well-done, defined 43

Yields from raw beef 9

RECIPE INDEX

Beef and Wild Mushroom Stroganoff 63

Beef Chili, Texas Style 76

Beef Cooked in Broth, Japanese Style 80

Beef Stock 72

Belgian Beef and Beer Stew 89

Borscht 75

Braised Beef Bundles 83

California Ranch Oven Stew 84

Carbonnade de Boeuf 89

Carne en Salsa Roja 79

Carpaccio 14

Casserole, Southern Beef and Noodle 48

Chili con Carne 76

Chili, New Mexico Style 79

Texas Style 76

Chuckwagon Meatloaf 47

Cilantro Salsa 33

Cocktail Patty Melts 20

Corn Pie in Ground Beef Crust 50

Corn-Stuffed Steak 24

Fajitas, Grilled Steak 26

Farsumagru 91

Fiery Orange Beef, Hunan Style 68

Fried Walnuts 23

Garlic Marinade 33

Garlic Steak Sandwich with Cilantro Salsa 33

Grilled Steak Fajitas 26

Grilled Steak with Peanut Sauce 29

Hamburgers 38

Hot Louisiana Meat Pies 52

Hot Raw Beef with Fresh Arugula 17

Kabobs, Middle Eastern 32

Korean Barbecued Beef 31

Kway Tieow Paht Si-yu 66

Marinade 24, 26, 29, 31, 32, 33

Meatballs 75

Meatloaf, Chuckwagon 47

Middle Eastern Kabobs 32

Minced Beef with Crisp Greens 65

Mustard Sauce 14

Panfried Steak 56

Pastel de Carne con Elote 50

Patty Melts, Cocktail 20

Peanut Sauce 29

Picadillo 86

Pies, Hot Louisiana Meat 52

Pot Roast with Root Vegetables 92

Red Chili Beef, New Mexico Style 79

Roast Tenderloin with Assorted Peppercorns 44

Root Vegetables, Pot Roast with 92

Salad, Sweet and Tangy Beef 23

Sandwich, Garlic Steak 33

Sautéed Steak Scallops with Herbed Mustard Sauce 58

Sautéed Tournedos with Fontina and Truffles 61

Seasoning Mixture 92

Shabu Shabu 80

Siberian Borscht with Meatballs 75

Sicilian Stuffed Beef Roll 91

Sliced Raw Beef Appetizers 14

South American Spicy Beef Stew 86

Southern Beef and Noodle Casserole 48

Spicy Ground Beef Patties 36

Stew, Belgian Beef and Beer 89

California Ranch Oven 84

South American Spicy Beef 86

Stock, Beef 72

Stroganoff, Beef and Wild Mushroom 63

Sweet and Tangy Beef Salad 23

Tartare, Western Steak 12

Thai Beef with Rice Noodles 66

Western Steak Tartare 12

ACKNOWLEDGMENTS

To Naomi's Antiques in San Francisco for locating so many of the nostalgic cowboy dishes.

To Dandelion retailers and Tampopo wholesalers in San Francisco for loaning innovative ironware.

To Carl Latino for the use of his western motif designs.

To the Ames Gallery in Berkeley for the use of Early American serving utensils.

To Bull's restaurant for the cow-shaped iron plate.

To those who loaned props or backgrounds from their personal collections of western memorabilia: D. Arvid Adams, John Carr, Carl Croft, Steve Fletcher, Jim Maclean, Scott McBride, Alan May, Dick and Lucille Owen, and Jerry Tokugawa.

To Roy Rogers and Gene Autry, who filled my childhood with fantasies of life on the range. Little did I know back then that it would be a cooking range.

To Peter Baumgartner, Aylett Cotton, Barbie Knecht, Martha McNair, and John Richardson for sharing some of their favorite recipes.

To Mary Ryan of the California Beef Council for providing reference materials.

To the staff of Chronicle Books for finally allowing me to add this book to my series and for letting me have my way with words and design most of the time.

To Sharon Silva for her superb copy editing.

To Glenn Carroll for assisting me in the kitchen with beef as the only remuneration.

To Patricia Brabant for another outstanding job behind the camera. And to her assistants Bruce Bennett and Carrie Loyd for all their help.

To my support group of family and friends who help me through my book projects in so many ways, especially to my sister Martha McNair, her husband John Richardson, and the world's greatest nephew, Devereux McNair.

To Addie Prey, Buster Booroo, Joshua J. Chew, Michael T. Wigglebutt, and Dweasel Pickle, all of whom love beef and were willing taste-testers while I developed recipes. And to Nelson Brabant who assumed this task during photography sessions.

To Lin Cotton, who, in addition to urging me to do this book, also loves the old cowboy song "Don't Fence Me In" and taught me its true meaning.